C0-ASL-800

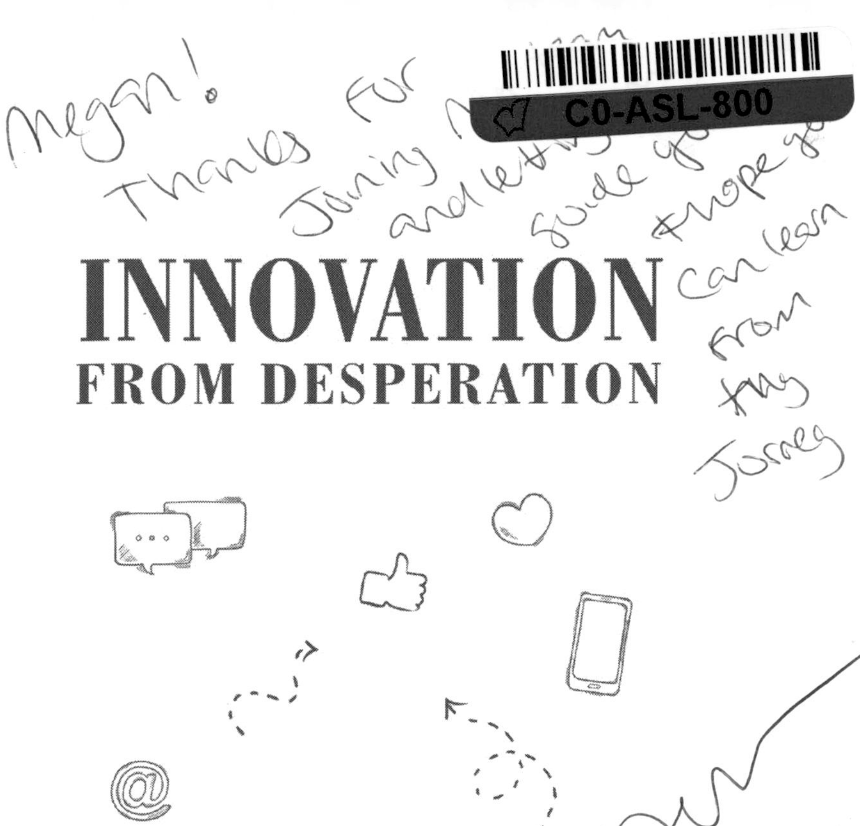

INNOVATION FROM DESPERATION

THE UNFILTERED FAILURES AND SUCCESSES OF AN OG SOCIAL MEDIA MARKETER

DESIREE MARTINEZ

PRAISE FOR THE AUTHOR

"If you're going after the life you want by starting a business, trust in Desiree Martinez. "Innovation From Desperation" is an honest, informative, and relatable guide that will give you the kick-in-the-pants many of us need to make moves towards a big and bright future. Desiree shows what it takes to position yourself as a trusted professional, while first highlighting the importance of trusting in your abilities and yourself."

-Amy Landino, Founder & CEO of GATLUW House

"Real, honest, and full of truth bombs — Desiree provides actionable insight that transcends industry or job title. A must-read for anyone looking for some extra innovation on their entrepreneurial journey!

- Russ Perry, Founder & CEO of Design Pickle

"You won't find a more candid, raw and inspirational look into what it takes to be a successful social media manager. Through her own story of ups and downs, Desiree Martinez reminds us that each failure is yet another opportunity to learn, adapt and grow. A must-read for anyone looking to start a social media business."

-- Gavin Hammar, CEO and Founder of Sendible

"Desiree Martinez takes readers on a relatable, heartfelt journey through her honest and fresh writing. Together, we travel with her from desperation to innovation. She shows all of us that you don't have to always have things figured out to start the road to entrepreneurship, marriage or motherhood in order to live the life of your dreams!"

- Sharon Bondurant, Founder & CEO of The Finders

“What Desiree shares in "Innovation From Desperation" is the perfect combination of real-life stories and professional experience, with a flare of honesty and humor. If you're seeking encouragement and wisdom to trust your instincts and go "out on your own," this is a must-read!”
–Meredith Marsh, Vid Pro Mom

“Finally, someone is actually telling the hard, honest truth about how difficult it is to be a mom and wife while owning their own business. Desiree does a fantastic job of cutting through all of the BS and getting REAL with her audience, so that we can hear the advice that can help us solve and get through the struggles we face as women entrepreneurs. This is 100% the book I and my fellow lady bosses need going forward to navigate through our own failures, struggles and victories so we can kick some business butt.”

- Crystal Hammon, CEO of Sitter for your Critter

“Reading Desiree’s book, I laughed out loud, got teary eyed and seriously inspired. Everyone can learn some great lessons from this book. Maybe failure isn’t so bad after all!”

- Devin Weber, CEO Braille Skateboarding

Innovation from Desperation: The unfiltered failures and successes of an OG Social Media Marketer

Copyright© 2020 by Pink Media, LLC

All rights reserved.

Edited by Dave Ficere,

Published by Pink Media, LLC
www.mrsdesireerose.com

Printed in the United States of America

ISBN: 978-0-578-70422-7

All rights reserved. Except in the case of brief quotations embodied in critical articles and reviews, no portion of this book may be reproduced, stored in a retrieval system, or transmitted in any form or by any means—electronic, mechanical, photocopy, recording, scanning, or other—without the prior written permission from the author. None of the material in this book may be reproduced for any commercial promotion, advertising or sale of a product or service.

For my mom, Jennifer.

Thank you for letting me fail, giving me ideas, and supporting me no matter what.

Innovation takes support and I know I always have that in you.

Thank you. I love you.

CONTENTS

FORWARD

As a gal who has a severe love/hate relationship with social media and in Desiree's own words, "Tisha, you've failed at every single platform except one," I know a thing or two about going from desperation to innovation. Rather than steering away from social media (cold hard fact: it's not going anywhere anytime soon), instead I learned to embrace it and use it the way I intended – to be authentically me.

When I first met Desiree back in 2012, I was running my former business, The Mom-e Club, and hosting my signature event, The Mom Entrepreneur of the Year awards. I was also running two other businesses in marketing and events management simultaneously with two small children. I was a complete nutcase! But I never let the world in to see that.

I looked at Desiree and thought to myself, "Now this girl has her shit together!" Her life appeared to be so well put together. Little did I know she hadn't yet entered into wife or mamahood yet, but she was about to find out.

I tried so hard to be the picture perfect, super successful mom entrepreneur all the time and it was well, let's say, completely exhausting and full of icky ick. Women who were 20, even 30 years older than I was had deemed me their "role model" and thrown me up on a pedestal making it even more impossible to keep up with the lies of perfection. I desperately wanted to come down and tell them my life was not all champagne and roses. It really was a hot mess 90% of the time. But I freaked out and kept digging myself deeper in the hole.

Until my 38th birthday, September 15, 2017.

I had just exited the year of hell. Age 37 when I decided to go bold, and bold meant going live on my personal Facebook profile.

Once the camera was rolling, I poured my heart out to the world that 2017 was going down as my shit year and I was going to light that baby on fire. Parents divorcing, best friends divorcing, involved in a money laundering scam unbeknownst to me, a failing business, marriage crumbling, kids misbehaving, broke, all confidence lost. Yep, what'd I tell you? No one was happier to see 37 go bye bye. You can watch it here at http://bit.ly/light37onfire.

You'd expect if you were going to come clean and cry on a live feed that you'd be judged from head to toe. And maybe there were some who asked, "what the hell is she doing?", but instead, I got the best thing ever...love and acceptance for all my flaws and the hot mess of a life. Hearts, thumbs up, comments, likes and it truly opened up my eyes that social media doesn't have to be the devil. It is the place to be the only person you need to be...YOU.

From that point on I experimented what platform was best suited for me and found that LinkedIn is my LOVE and I've been incredibly active and engaged since January 2018 when I decided that I was no longer hiding behind the mask. I was going to speak whatever was on my mind, be engaging, ask thought provoking questions, be visible and create community.

Since making social media more a part of my life, especially using video which I highly recommend, I've seen tremendous personal growth, business success and opportunities up the wazoo from being featured in several podcasts, getting booked for speaking engagements, building my Social Connect PHX tribe, launching a live stream and so much more. It's caused me to think outside the box, ask for guidance and surround myself with even more mentors and role models globally.

I know deep down, it can do the exact same for you, just as it has done for me, and Desiree.

Believe me. She and I? We get it. We've been there. We've ugly cried together. We've talked each other off the so-called entrepreneurial ledge. We've invested in each other's dreams and insane "will this work" ideas multiple times, and if there is one person on this entire planet who will tell you straight what getting to the sweet spot of success is, it's her.

I cannot wait for you to dive into this book, learn from Desiree, and read firsthand how this OG social media marketer went from desperation to innovation and how she did it. I LOVE THIS GIRL for never giving up on her dreams, her family, her friends and wanting the absolute best for every person she meets.

Desiree, YOU DID IT!!! I know this book did not come easy to write, but the hard part is now over. Celebrating you, my ride or die friend! Thank you for being authentically you, sharing your story with the world and empowering even more individuals to keep on keeping on just as you did. (Checking "guest write in someone's book" off my bucket list!)

Much love,
Tisha Marie Pelletier
@tishamariepelletier

SHARE YOUR JOURNEY!

This book dives into some deep stuff and at the end of each chapter you will find the "Moment of Innovation" where you can share your related story with me.

Just post on social media with hashtag **#ShareYourInnovation** on your favorite social network.

When you share your image or story, you'll be entered to win a free one-on-one content strategy session with me, Desiree Martinez. I will pick one per month for as long as this hashtag is shared!

Thanks for reading and sharing with me.

CHAPTER 1
DOING ALL THE RIGHT THINGS

The movie "Toy Story" was released on November 22, 1995. It was a day that totally changed my life.

I was ten when my parents took me to see the landmark movie, which was the first entirely computer-animated feature film. It was also the first feature film from Pixar. I don't remember anything about the theater, what I wore or any other details. I do remember my response to my parents' question about whether I liked the movie. As we walked back to the car, I told them, "I want to do that when I grow up!"

By that, I meant I wanted to be an animator for Pixar. I wanted to tell amazing stories and touch the lives of everyone who entered that magical world of a movie theater. I wanted to inspire them through beautiful and believable art. Even now as an adult with all my logic and knowledge, I still secretly hope that my toys will come to life when I leave the room. I make sure to instill this whimsy and wishful thinking into my own kids.

Unlike most kids who waver about what to do in their future, I did not. I stayed steadfast, with my eye on this same goal of becoming a Pixar animator. I studied hard all through middle and high school so that I could get into the college of my choice. Initially, I thought I wanted to go to UCLA because they had some type of 3-D art program. However, with the help of my dad I ended up at The Art Institute of Colorado, which was also close to home. Just in case I needed some extra support!

My dad always taught me to work hard and never settle for "average." He always challenged me by never accepting my best as the best I could do. I once came home with a report card of all "As." His response? He looked at me and said, "But can you do it again?" No doubt after I tell him I am writing this book, he will say something like, "But is it a best-seller?"

Desiree Ford holds up her favorite Disney movie. Ever since she was young, she has wanted to be in on the action of making a Pixar production. She plans on attending the Art Institute of Denver to fulfill this dream. Photo by Julia Watson

You might think he was overly strict. But he set a high standard, and that is something that has stuck with me. I can't settle for just being good, I have to be great. And I made for damn sure that I was great after high school. All I did through college was work and sleep. My homework and projects always came first, which I know is a total buzzkill! But this tenacity allowed me to graduate Cum Laude and with the second-best portfolio in my class. I was proud to finish second, because the student that was first totally deserved it! They had an amazing portfolio.

Not only do I never settle, but I am also a planner. I knew that in order to get a job and stand out from my peers I would need to be aggressive in my job search. One month before I graduated, there was a huge gaming conference in San Francisco. I knew that if I could get in with a gaming studio, it would put me on the path of career success. I wouldn't just be some resume in the pile. Rather, I would be a person they knew and liked. I actually asked my family to get me a brand new piece of tech called the iPod Video for Christmas so I could put my demo reel on it and take it to the Game Developers Conference to show recruiters, developers, and anyone who would talk with me what I was capable of.

I had a plan, a plane ticket, a reservation at a super sketchy but cheap hotel, a pass to the conference, and my demo reel on my new shiny iPod Video. I knew I could not and would not fail!

Everyone was really impressed to see my demo reel on the iPod and dozens of studios gave me their cards and told me "when you graduate send your resume and demo reel DVD and we will talk."

I was on cloud nine! All those years of working hard, sacrificing party time, money, and a personal life were paying off! After graduation, with my diploma in hand, I started reaching out to all those companies, mailing my resume and demo reel (that's how we did it back then), and followed up with an email.

Crickets.

When I was finally able to get a hold of someone, I began hearing the same things over and over. "We aren't hiring," "the studio is shutting down," "we only had enough budget for this one game."

I was confused and bummed out, but I pushed on.

I kept applying. Everywhere. With the same results. Over and over. I took art test after art test just to be told, "No," because of funding, or should I say, lack of funding. Companies were just folding, jobs weren't available, and worse, I was now competing for entry level jobs with other 3D artists who had experience.

That was 2007. The economy was about to completely implode and opportunities for everyone were about to go away.

Completely mortified, I ended up moving back in with my parents in 2009. Like so many other college graduates, I started looking for work doing anything. All those years of hard work, dedication, and dreaming had been for nothing, I thought. Yes, you could argue that I learned a lot about hard work, networking and blah blah blah. I didn't care. I wanted a job doing what I loved. What I had trained for. What I had been dreaming of since I was ten years old.

I thought back to high school. There was a picture in my Senior yearbook of me holding a VHS tape of Toy Story and a caption of me talking about my dream of being a Pixar animator. I wanted it badly then and I truly believed that if I worked hard and got good grades that I would get what I wanted.

I did everything right. I was the one my teachers, professors, department heads, and friends never worried about. They always told me I was talented and driven and hungry. More so than anyone else they knew. "You're going to be just fine," they all said. Instead, I was back living in my parents' spare room, making less than ten-dollars an hour selling business cards to doctors, lawyers, and dentists. I didn't even get to design any of them. I was just selling them. I was at rock bottom.

While dad is my motivator, my mother is my cheerleader. She is always looking for unique ways to help me. Once she handed me a newspaper listing all the millionaire women who owned companies in the Phoenix area. She suggested that I reach out to each of them to congratulate them and give them a soft pitch about myself. I took the paper and pitched the idea to the business card company I was working for. Since they were desperate for business, they allowed me to print 200 cards and paid for the postage. I spent a week putting together a spreadsheet of names, websites, companies, and addresses, writing letters, and mailing them out.

While I got a couple thank you notes and a handful of "unable to deliver" letters, one person wrote back to me. She was the owner of a tech recruiting company. She said she really admired my hustle and "had to meet me." We met for coffee. Well, tea for me (you should know that every time I talk about coffee, I always mean tea). We hit it off, and ever since then, she has been my mentor and friend. To this day, I do social media and graphic design work for her.

All this happened because of my mama.

So, when my mom sent me a link to a website called NetworkingPhoenix.com and told me to find free events to go to and try to hawk my design skills, I listened. "What did I have to lose?" was really my mentality by this time because I was desperate.

I remember my first event. It was a breakfast mastermind meeting at a restaurant down the street that my family loved. I was hands down the youngest person in the filled-to-capacity room. I sat down and shook the hands of the people next to me and just listened. I don't remember the message, but I do remember that this was unlike anything I had ever been to. People were everywhere, talking, laughing, and exchanging business cards. When Dave, the leader, stood up to take his time in the spotlight to lead the group and give his message, everyone listened and followed along on the paper he handed out.

Then we did something really weird. We went around the room. Everyone stood up and told the group about their business and what services and value they could bring to the rest of us if we were interested in talking with them. My eye bugged out of my head. Like, "What the what?" I had so many questions.

Is this for real?

Was I expected to do business with all these people?

Talk to all these people?

Could I get all of them to use me for their graphic design needs?

What was I going to say when it was my turn? "Hi, I'm Desiree, art school failure desperate for money hoping that you will pay me to do any design work you need done?"

I am not a shy person and I've got the performing monkey thing down, but it was really how I felt. It was a mix of emotions from excitement to uncertainty. But what did I have to lose?

I took some time to talk with people, exchange business cards, and then went home. I emailed the people I had talked with giving them a little bit of information about me and my hourly rate of $12 per hour for graphic design work. TWELVE DOLLARS! (Can we all facepalm together for a moment)?

They all responded nicely and said they would keep me in mind if they needed anything.

I told my mom about what happened and she just smiled in her mom way and told me to keep trying. She said the more I put myself out there, eventually I would find someone who needed my help or they would know about me when they needed me.

Again, what did I have to lose?

I kept going back to that breakfast mastermind group because Dave had said that the more you show up at events, then the more people will know they can count on you. You also begin building relationships. Then he dropped the magic line that rings true for everything and everyone in business: "People do business with those they know, like, and trust."

I had never heard that before. Remember, I had spent my whole life preparing to work for someone else. My mantra had always been to work hard and you will get the things you want. It just never occurred to me that hard work alone wouldn't result in the things I wanted. This was a lightbulb moment. It was the first time I was realizing that hard work means nothing if you don't find the right people to work for or with.

I kept going to "stuff," or rather networking events, as they were called. I would dress-up, smile, shake hands, learn about people, exchange business cards, do coffee meetups, and just keep trying to find people to do business with. And I did convert some of them into clients. Others told me my $12 per hour fees were too high (yep, that happened). I heard a LOT of pitches for different network marketing businesses, and made some really great friends.

One day I was at a Starbucks with a man named Kevin. He helped business professionals develop leadership skills and agreed to meet with me, probably to vet me for his program. As I sat down, he asked me, "Do you know what this Facebook thing is?"

I looked at him stunned, and a little confused. I had been on Facebook since 2006. Back then, you could only get on with a college email. I used it to stay connected with my roommates from my study abroad program. Later, Facebook allowed me to stay connected with my classmates as they began migrating to it and away from MySpace. I sat there thinking about my Facebook photo album. It celebrated Italy winning the World Cup circa 2006, showcasing my summer college clothing attire along with a lot of booze. I'm thinking, what is this old man asking about Facebook for?

But I politely told him, "Yes, I know about Facebook" and told him my PG experience with it. He told me that he had received an invite to join, and wanted to know how he could use it for business. So, I told him how he could "Friend" his family and networking friends, and post about what he was doing in his business on the News Feed. Then, I continued, if he really wanted to get serious, he could make a "Fan Page," where anyone who "Liked" his page would get information from him about his business. Even if they didn't personally know him.

He was excited, but a little overwhelmed. He pulled out his laptop and asked me more questions, which I answered. After his excitement died down, he turned to me and said, "You should do this for a business!"

I looked at him with a deadpan expression on my face. With every serious fiber of my being I replied, "No one is going to pay to be on Facebook."

After we finished our meeting, I went home and talked to my mom. I told her about my meeting and how Kevin told me about doing Facebook for business. My mom had recently joined the Facebook world and was loving reconnecting with her old friends and family. So, when she said, "Well, why not? What do you have to lose?" It made me really take pause and think about it.

Was this actually an option? Was this college student social network really a place I could make money?

I am a child of the 90s, one who grew up with a computer in my home since 1992. We had America on Line (AOL) in 1994 and I remember how excited I was when I got to play an online game called "Boogers." I remember taking typing class in middle school as a part of PE, but not being allowed to use the Internet to write papers because the information couldn't be trusted! I downloaded songs from Napster (remember them?) to make my own custom burned CDs under my super sweet DJ name "White Jockey Jams" for all my friends. No judgment please. I really thought I was SO cool. Besides, we all have a past!

MySpace and Facebook were made for people JUST LIKE ME. Those of us who remember our first cell phones in high school or college but still understood how to use a payphone. Kids who were now adults who grew as the Internet blossomed. We were the first generation who you could say were being trained and educated for jobs that didn't exist yet, especially in regards to the Internet.

Facebook was such a huge deal in 2008 because

Chris Cox, one of its co-founders, joined the Barack Obama Presidential campaign. Facebook really helped show how social media could be used to effect change and policy decisions in America and around the world. In contrast, MySpace had been all about connecting with friends, creating an online place that represented you, showing off your style and favorite music. You could also know who someone's true friends were with your Top 8. I remember taking on freelance work to design MySpace pages for brands who were interested in being where all the kids were. And, back then, that is where all the kids were.

So, could it be possible that this idea of making money by being on Facebook and helping others do so could actually work?

As it turns out, this wasn't a new idea. There were already dozens of companies that did Search Engine Optimization (SEO), blogging, website design, and online advertising. Many of them were offering clients Facebook and Twitter management as an option. They would create a Facebook Fan Page and a Twitter account for brands and then write posts about that business. Hopefully, people would flock to those websites and buy their products.

Hand to God, this is exactly what people were "promising" back in the old days of Facebook and that is sort of how it worked. Algorithms weren't nearly the pain in the ass that they are now. There weren't over two billion people using Facebook and more than 60 million Facebook Business pages fighting for users' attention. It really was simple: You created a Facebook Page and people actually saw it and responded.

I know I can do this, I thought. This is what is going to allow me to stand out. This is going to be my professional future. Now I just had to figure out how to do it.

MOMENT OF INSPIRATION

What do you have to lose? I thought.

I said that a lot to myself during this time in my life. I was at rock bottom, so I really didn't have anything to lose, but that is something you have to ask yourself anyway. What do you have to lose by trying something new, especially when it comes to your social media?

Maybe you lose some time?
Some money?
You look silly?

But what if you turn that question around? Ask yourself, what would I lose if I DIDN'T do this? Could you miss out on a money-making opportunity? A connection with someone who could be a partner, a friend, or a lover? By not being on Social Media you could be missing out more than money. You might miss out on a life-changing connection. More about that a little bit later…

What's also really amazing about the "what do I have to lose?" mentality is that whether you sink or swim, you learn. You will learn so much. I spent thousands of dollars and years of my life on my college education. All to pursue a dream I had since my childhood, a dream that completely failed. And when I look back at that time, I can definitely say while going to college is one of the biggest regrets of my life, I did learn some things.

I learned about digital art, graphic design, and what makes a good website. College taught me how to use video cameras, composition, and tools to design the things I wanted to make. I also learned about networking, how to stand out, and what I can do. I am capable of so much and so are you! So, stop doubting yourself, questioning everything, and asking is it worth it. Just say "What do I have to lose?"

Tag me with me your "What do I have to lose?" moment @mrsdesireerose with #shareyourinspiraiton on social media.

CHAPTER 2
I HAVE NO IDEA WHAT I'M DOING

Becoming what we now call a Social Media Manager quickly became my new obsession. I didn't have time to ease into it. I needed to make money, and get the "f" out of my parents' house, 'cause fur realz, I was over living there! (I love you mom and dad, but we need our own living spaces.)

I started reading everything I could find about Facebook Fan Pages, Twitter, Linkedin, Friendster, and how businesses could use the Internet to generate new leads. I started learning about Search Engine Optimization (SEO), email marketing, blogging, and everything about the Internet associated with business use. I found amazing resources and insights on Mashable.com and SocialMediaExaminer.com, but I knew I needed to test what I was learning.

The problem with any new business venture is the j.o.b. That is, generating income while launching a new venture. And that was a problem for me, because the business card company I was working for had to lay me off. They didn't have the money to keep me on. Plus, I had started a new job as a personal assistant to a real hustler, a focused guy who ran "job-seeker" conventions. He was also dabbling in launching an expo series around energy. It was a really interesting time, and the coolest thing that came out of that opportunity was getting free box seats to see WrestleMania XXVI at Cardinal Stadium in Phoenix. I got to take my new boyfriend, who was a huge wrestling fan. Score one for me!

But that was the only cool thing about the job. This guy ended up selling his convention business a month after hiring me. Part of the deal with the new owner was I would do the work. So, I now had to put together a job seekers conference, which in 2010 was just stupid. Unemployment in the U.S. was at an all-time high, and companies weren't short on finding applicants for jobs. So why would they pay to come to a job fair? Exactly, they wouldn't.

It sucked. I was working 10-plus hour days, driving 45 minutes each way to the office, and getting continuous pressure from my boss to perform. I tried, and I tried, and nothing was happening. It was just a business model that didn't make sense anymore. Needless to say, that job ended after six-weeks, and the new owner dissolved the company she had just bought.

Through these weird jobs, there was one thing that stayed the same. I kept networking and figuring out how to be a social media manager. I continued meeting with people, teaching them about Facebook, helping them set up accounts, and showing them how to use social media to connect and share. Slowly, I began positioning myself as the only social media professional anyone knew.

So jobless, yet again, I needed to figure out how to make money from this social media thing. In between freelance gigs, I was testing out this new app called Foursquare. It was a location check-in app where you would go somewhere, check-in, earn badges, and get deals. It told your friends in their app news feed where you were and connected to Facebook and Twitter. Foursquare represented another opportunity to continue sharing with my growing network about what I was doing, and "being cool" on a new social network.

I really liked the app and the community that was being built around it. I decided I was going to become the leading resource on all things Foursquare. I figured as the "official Foursquare expert," I would be taken more seriously and draw more businesses to work with me. I was able to use my love of the app to become a Level 3 Super User, which meant I could edit location check-ins for my area. And, as a bonus, I headed up the first-ever Foursquare Day with Meetup.com. Foursquare even sent me some fun swag to share with the ten people that showed up.

With this new Foursquare power, I was going to sell a package deal to brick and mortar locations. I would set them up on Foursquare with their precise location and also get them correctly set up on Facebook and Twitter. That meant making sure they had a username, their "about" info all filled out, yadda yadda. And, my big upsell was providing 60-days of content generation for them.

Sweet deal, huh!

I didn't sell a single one. People liked the idea of being cutting edge, but putting money behind it didn't make sense to them. Some of the excuses I got, included:

- I can just have my kid set this up for me
- I don't understand how this will make me any money
- I can't track these conversions
- Why would I pay you when I can do this myself?
- I'd rather spend money on something I understand
- Why would I pay for something that is free?

It sucked to keep being told no, but these "nos" allowed me to figure out how to respond to get them to say "yes" eventually.

Dennis Crowley - Founder of Foursquare

Dennis Crowley is the co-founder and Executive Chairman of Foursquare, the technology platform that powers location experiences for more than 1 billion people around the world. He is also the founder and Chairman of the Kingston Stockade Football Club, a semi-professional soccer team out of Hudson Valley, NY that competes in the 4th division of the US Soccer Pyramid.

I had a company before Foursquare, called Dodgeball. Both of them were playground games. Dodgeball came about in the early 2000s because I worked at a dot com company, it was like my second job out of school, and I got laid off. When I was laid off, I was in New York, and most of my friends got laid off from their jobs also. We built, well, I built a piece of software and called it Dodgeball, and it was designed to let you know where your laid-off friends are so you can meet up with them and have a drink.

Later, Google expressed interest in our thesis project, which we were trying to turn into a company, and so they bought it. We went to Google and worked there for two years. We built a whole bunch of stuff, but I didn't really get to do as much as I wanted. I left Google, and then Google, in turn, was going to turn Dodgeball off, which we still used to meet up with our friends.

When they decided to turn it off, we said, "We'll make another one, and we'll call it Foursquare." It wasn't meant to be a company. It wasn't meant to be this thing that I'd work on for 10 or 12 years. It was just like, "Hey, our friends use this software that helps them meet up at bars and parks around the city. There are people in other cities that use it. If Google was going to turn it off, we'd make them another one." That's kind of how it started.

During my crappiest, laid-off moment, my mom gave me advice, which was the classic mom advice of "do what you love, and the rest will come." I was like, "I just like making software for my friends. I like to make stuff that people use." Many times, it doesn't make any sense, and if you work on it long enough, sometimes it starts to make sense to a large audience.

Foursquare blew-up in part by the adamant users, like Desiree, who were eager to crowdsource the locations of places all over their cities. This was the secret sauce of Foursquare's success. The community was just amazing and I couldn't have asked for a better group of enthusiastic Super Users (what we called our editing community.) Eventually, Foursquare capped out its user base, and with many of the other big social networks copying our technology, we had to get innovative and adapt. Now Foursquare is used as one of the largest location experiences for more than 1 billion people around the world.

I hope a whole lot of friends are using it to meet up and get drinks.

MOMENT OF INNOVATION

The two pieces of advice I'd give you is, number one, I'm going to reiterate my mom's advice, which is do what you love, and the rest will come. When you are in the middle

> of the shittiest moments of your career, that's really crappy advice. But, at some point, it becomes relevant, because you do find something that you like. I do have a job that I enjoy now and you can, too.
>
> And the second piece of advice that I give to people all the time is, if there is something in the world that you wish existed, instead of waiting for someone else to make it, just go make it yourself.

Making It Official

It was during this time I came across this article on Mashable about how they were partnering with Meetup.com to create Social Media Day. This day would "acknowledge and celebrate the revolution of media becoming social. A day that honors the technological and societal advancements that have allowed us to have a dialogue, to connect and to engage not only the creators of media, but perhaps more importantly, one another."

Reading this nowadays would make most people go, "big whoop." But in 2010, this was gigantic, especially for lil' ole me, who was quickly becoming obsessed with social media. I was going to make it official. Not just Facebook official, either, I am talking legally official.

After much deliberation on my couch, with my mom, and polling my growing Facebook friends list, I was legally going to become Pink Media L.L.C. I was going to make the world a better place by helping businesses build and execute their social media strategy. And, on June 30, 2010, the first-ever Social Media Day, I officially went into business for myself.

I was pumped and had absolutely no idea what I was doing. I took solace in a couple of things:

Social Media was new to the "normal" world, and there was no playbook for it yet. So, it was okay that I was figuring out how to use it for business.

As a society, we were still recovering from the Great Recession. People, just like me, were trying to figure things out for themselves, and how they were going to make money.

I was going to hear "no" a LOT! But I realized that, and knew their "noes" were going to help me get to the "yesses." All I needed to figure out what to do for these businesses to get them to say yes.

MOMENT OF INSPIRATION

Some things (and some people) never change. Those excuses I kept getting from people not signing up for my service? I STILL get told these exact things from people as to why they don't want to utilize what I offer. It doesn't matter how good of an answer you give them, how right you are, or how much you can help their business. Some people just don't want to do it. This is a hard pill to swallow, but think about yourself. What is something that you haven't done because you didn't want to pay for it or you thought you could do it yourself? In the end, you probably wish you had just paid someone to do it for you.

There is a saying I love that I saw for the first time on the side of someone's car. It said:

"If you think paying an expert is expensive, just wait until you hire an amateur."

Let that sink in.

I can't tell you how many clients I have that have come to me because they can't get access to their social media accounts that were set up by a former employee. Or they lost their website because they decided to stop working with a particular web company. They took the website with them when they left and are now clueless. Or, it might be something as simple as they don't have a high-resolution image of their logo because their graphic designer never gave it to them, or they can't get a hold of the person who designed it.

I am not saying that you need to throw money to

the wind and hire the most expensive person, but working with the right expert will almost always yield better results. When it comes to your social media, remember you are going to have to invest if you want it done right. Even if you are a marketer, you are still going to have to shell out money, or time (which is another form of currency) to manage your online presence.

It is ok if you don't know what to do or are struggling to keep up with it all, that's why people like me exist. What is most important is that you invest in yourself and your business or brand to accomplish the things you want. I basically had no life while I was trying to figure out what I was doing, but in the long run it paid off, but not without some big mistakes along the way.

What was ground zero for you on your journey? Share your origins story with my by tagging me @mrsdesireerose with #shareyourinspiration on social media.

CHAPTER 3
LEARNING THE HARD WAY

On my way to figuring out what the heck a social media professional was and what to offer businesses, I made some pretty big mistakes along the way.

What sucks most about these mistakes is that they sting the most when you are first starting out. That is when you are the most impressionable, vulnerable, gullible, and can least afford to make mistakes financially. I had some doozies, and in the full disclosure of being transparent about my failures, I am sharing my biggest ones with you.

The Arizona Pop Culture Museum

Y'all know by now how supportive and helpful my

mother is. In my early days, she knew that I was trying to educate myself excessively about the online marketing space. She had found a free SEO class through the library and sent the info my way. Naturally, I went.

The class was basic, but what mattered the most was who was there. We were all given a chance to talk about why we were attending and what we did. As we went around the room, there was one guy, James*, that stood out. He was there to learn about SEO to help a non-profit he ran, called The Arizona Pop Culture Museum (AZPCM).

The AZPCM was a museum with over 10,000 collector edition toys that were still in mint condition. The museum was located in a struggling shopping center and gave five-dollar tours. Their number one challenge was the lack of public awareness about them and minimal foot traffic.

This was the PERFECT challenge for me! I am a HUGE nerd. My best friend and I were founders of a Meetup.com group called N.E.R.D.S., where we brought people together around the common theme of nerd and pop culture. We went to movies, local comic cons, partnered with costume groups like the 501st (Star Wars cosplayers) and The Browncoat (Joss Whedon/Firefly fans). We did charity events and would hang out, watch anime, go to ren faire, and were the hub for all things nerdy to do in Phoenix. We even launched pop culture debates pinning the biggest fandoms against each other. They would fight it out over which was better: Star Wars vs. Star Trek, Harry Potter vs. Lord of the Rings, Marvel vs. DC. You get the idea.

We redefined nerdom in Phoenix and became a safe haven for nerds to let their flags fly when being a nerd was still not trendy. But what's better is that my husband and I met at a Zombieland movie meetup on October 3, 2009. But for the sake of this story, the husband (Stephen) is my boyfriend.

So back to AZPCM. After talking with James about the museum, I realized I had to check it out. Once I walked in, I knew I HAD to work with them. James was a textbook old school nerd. Glasses, balding, wearing comic book shirts, and friendly. He loved pop culture and had single-handedly bought the more than 10,000 toys showcased at the museum. He had quite a financial investment in something he loved.

After taking the tour, we talked about what he wanted to accomplish for his museum and how I could help him. His biggest need was getting the word out about his museum. He had no idea how to do it because he came from a music production background, and marketing was awkward for him. However, I spoke nerd, had zero problems talking with people, and was looking to make a name for myself. I offered him my services for free because I needed a test case to display my skills. The museum would be my first client, and I couldn't have been more excited.

I was also able to get Stephen a paid job there as a docent. He was also a huge nerd and loved everything the museum offered. He knew between his nerd knowledge, my growing connections and skills, and our combined brainstorming, we were going to make this museum a must-see tourist destination in Arizona.

If that wasn't amazing enough, James sent Stephen and me to San Diego Comic-Con in his place. He could not attend because of a family obligation and told us to pick up that year's exclusive line of toys for him.

Seriously, I had made it! This was absolutely perfect and proved to me that I was definitely on the right path for my professional career! FINALLY, after years of just flailing away.

I crushed the project for James. I steadily grew his engaging social media presence and got AZPCM setup with the Greater Phoenix Chamber of Commerce. They even did a big networking event there. I was getting James into the local press, and, as a result, tours were increasing. Partnerships with all the costuming groups were in the planning stages, and I started to use social media to get his museum national attention. At that time, a cable TV station called G4 had a program entitled "Attack of the Show." They had a segment that highlighted cool nerdy places around the world, and I was working on getting the museum on that segment.

This is all great, right? How could this be listed as a failure for you, Desiree?

Well, here's the thing. Sometimes it doesn't matter how good of a job you do, because even the people you are helping can sabotage it. Through all the work I was doing, the recognition and popularity of the museum began to grow. Unfortunately, so did James's arrogance. He became overly confident and cocky, stopped listening to advice, and instead invested time and money into things that yielded no return. He hired an incredibly sweet and naive girl (who also happened to look just like a real-life Wonder Woman) as his personal assistant. Seriously, she was incredibly beautiful but knew NOTHING about pop culture However, she looked amazing in the Wonder Woman costume James bought, which was enough for him. (Yep, it was also like that).

He had decided to relocate the museum to a new area where there would be more foot traffic, a real opportunity for growth, and a reasonable price on a lease. We helped them move to the new location, which gave Stephen the chance to suggest doing a new temporary exhibit. He thought it would create fresh press buzz, encourage previous visitors to return, and increase the reach of fandom.

The museum's exhibits were "male-heavy," with full collections for Star Trek, Star Wars, GI Joe, Hot Wheels, and many more. Don't get me wrong, I am super feminist, and all about girl power and equality, but even I didn't grow up playing with any of these toys. Stephen gave countless tours at the museum with couples where the guy would be all chatty and pumped, and the girl would be clearly bored out of her mind.

Stephen suggested that we do a temporary exhibit with something like Barbie or Sanrio so that we could appeal to a broader (and more female) audience. James hated the idea purely because he didn't personally like those things. It didn't matter that we had presented him with the facts about Barbie being the most popular and profitable toy of all time. Or Sanrio, the creator of Hello Kitty, made more money annually than Mattel and Hasbro combined. He just said, "no one over the age of five cares about that stuff."

James also wanted to push for selling more t-shirts and comic books. He even considered getting rid of the museum altogether. Stephen tirelessly explained that the museum was what would attract new people and that a new exhibit would bring previous guests back. The store, he pointed out, was an additional revenue stream, and would help the museum to continue making money on an ongoing basis.

Stephen and James just kept butting heads. Ultimately, James fired both of us because he didn't like the vision Stephen had for the museum. James also wanted to give Stephen's job to Wonder Woman.

The lesson I learned was this: It doesn't matter how right you are if your customer won't listen to you or is too scared to move ahead. You will just be spinning your wheels. We loved the museum so much! We knew the potential it had and had grand plans to make it an amazing and true tourist destination. But, at the end of the day, our vision wasn't James's, which is still such a sore spot for Stephen.

What can you learn from this experience? When you are getting started in business or have a new offer or system you want to test, working for free is a great way to get some experience under your belt. Think of it as an investment in yourself. That is why stores will do Groupons and free days, and restaurants give out free samples. They want to see if what they're offering is any good.

However, you need to be really clear about what you are going to offer for free. Set expectations, limitations, and an end date. That way, you and the person you are working with know what is going on and when it will end. Hopefully, after they get a taste of what you can do for them, they will hire you.

As for making someone follow your suggestions

and listen to you when you KNOW you're right, well, that one is much harder. The best advice I can offer is to present them with the facts, your plan, and the reasons for it, and your projection of the results. With the museum, we presented them with the reality that museums continually change exhibits to keep people coming back. We gave them suggestions along with supporting data for top-performing products in the museum's genre. We showed James what press coverage and partnerships we could generate from a new exhibit and how that would increase traffic to the new museum location.

He said "no," and there was nothing I could do about it.

People say no, and that sucks, but you can't take it personally. Some clients or prospects are afraid to invest in things they don't understand. Their fear does not mean you don't know what you are talking about and that you can't do great things for them. It is, on their part, a fear of the unknown. But that is why they hire an expert (that would be YOU)!

It is so easy to think about what you've lost or will lose versus giving your all to something you have and believe in. There are people out there that will invest in you because they believe in you and what you can do. Give those people your brain space, ideas, and excitement. Don't dwell on those who live in fear or are too mentally constipated to grow from your vision.

Larry*

One of the things I excel at is finding good people to work with. It is not a natural gift, but a learned skill brought about by one person. I don't remember precisely how Larry came into my life, but he must have sensed my eagerness and desperation. He was ready to milk me for all I was worth.

Larry and I crossed paths when he was putting an event together for the food industry and needed a social media person. A mutual friend had recommended me, and I was happy to participate. Larry had this way of validating you while also making you wholeheartedly believe everything he was saying.

At this time, I had started creating Facebook Landing pages for brands, which are "Like Gates" for Facebook Fan pages. When you went to a Facebook Fan Page for the first time, rather than being faced with a feed of posts, you wound up on the Facebook Landing Page. Most Fan Pages offered an incentive to join. For example, a restaurant would say, "Like this page and get a free appetizer on your first visit." After the user "Liked" the page, the next page revealed the appetizer coupon and gave the reader information about the business. It was like a mini-website but on Facebook.

I had developed a simple way to modify code and

design so that it was easy to replicate for new customers and minimize the time I spent doing it. I would create Facebook Landing pages for clients as well as their Social Media Business Card (also known as their profile picture) as a part of a Facebook setup fee. Then, I would up-sell customers on 60-days' worth of social media postings. I charged $500 for this, and businesses really liked the idea because they understood that designing and coding took time, like building a "real" website. They were fine paying for it and were willing to take a chance on the postings.

There weren't many people in Phoenix doing this, so Larry liked my skill set. He took me under his wing and started having me go everywhere with him. Together, we attended countless meetings to educate his prospects about social media and why they needed it. Then as a follow-up, Larry would have a conversation with them, pitching them a package and pricing proposal. Magically, they became his clients, and I would start designing landing pages and writing posts for them.

I was his go-to person for social media, and I ways worked directly with him as a part of his tea This didn't bother me because he always paid r Meanwhile, I was continuing to hustle. I was j grinding day and night figuring out what the he was doing, trying to establish myself as the go-to soc media professional in town.

Innovation from Desperation

I looked at Larry as a mentor. We would meet and talk about business, ideas, and he would guide me on what to do to get the things I wanted. Usually, that meant, "stick with me! We are going to do great things together."

I ended up introducing Stephen to Larry because I talked about Larry so much, and he had become such a big part of my life, time, and income. But Stephen didn't like Larry, and that was really hard for me. It was the first time this had ever happened in our one-year-old relationship. My boyfriend had no other way to describe it other than "I just get a bad feeling about him." I was baffled and defensive. Larry had done so much for me and brought me so much business. How could he not be a good guy!

Then it happened. One day Larry asked me to show him how I made my Landing Pages. In my trusting nature, I showed him how I did it, where to put the code, and how I worked through my process.

After that, crickets.

Larry ignored every email, phone call, and text. Finally, I reached out to him through the friend that had connected us. She told me that he hired a college student to create landing pages and social media business cards for his clients because he could pay them less. He actually said, "why would I pay you $500 when I could pay someone less for the same amount of work."

He stole my process, my code, and betrayed my trust. I was heartbroken. And what was worse, is that the friend who had connected us desperately needed the money that he was paying her. As a result, I also lost my friend and thought she had betrayed me as well. (She eventually came back, and we remain friends to this day). She told me that he actually hijacked her email and was emailing me pretending to be her, and saying all kinds of terrible things about me!

I think it is important to note that I genuinely believe most people are good. I have met hundreds of wonderful people and have built my business off of being a good person willing to help people in any way I reasonably can. I am a connector, and I love helping people. Larry was a snake, but I'm not the first to be taken in. I am willing to bet if you were to ask any business owner about someone in their professional life who let them down or took advantage of them, they would all have a "Larry" story to tell.

What I want you to learn from this experience is that people are going to burn you, and it sucks, but it shouldn't stop you from continuing to do what you love. I still loved social media marketing even after the bad experience with Larry. I knew I wanted to keep going with it. I realized I just needed to be more mindful of the people I partnered with in business. I also would advise you to draw up contracts for every client and partner you have, which allows you to manage expectations with your clients. If it is all written out and agreed upon, then you can move forward with confidence in your relationships. Also, protect your systems and methods, and don't give away all your secrets.

I also want to note that my boyfriend (and now husband) Stephen always meets people I want to do big things with. Often, his gut feeling can tell me yes or no. So, if you are lucky enough to have a bullshit detector in your life, use them!

Arizona Pop Culture Museum, Part Two

Yep, there is a part two!

A year after we left the museum project, I was steadily growing my business. My boyfriend was working on his engineering degree at Arizona State University when he got a call from James. He wanted to meet with both of us.

After much deliberation, we agreed to a sit-down. The long and short of it was that James wanted us back. The museum had steadily slid into decline after we left, and he needed help. Wonder Woman was gone, and the museum had a new manager who knew about pop culture but knew nothing about business. The museum hadn't gotten any press, rent was going up, and foot traffic was way down.

He apologized for how things had gone before and asked if we would come back. After much deliberation, Stephen and I agreed to come back under the following conditions:

Stephen was made assistant manager and got a raise with the option to become a partner in the museum.

James would pay me for my time and work and trust my process.

James would agree to changing exhibits as other museums do.

James would also agree to let us plan events to keep traffic coming into the museum.

James accepted these conditions, and we continued forward.

James had been a collector for so long that he had been able to work out great deals with distribution companies for comic books and merchandise. Stephen had convinced James to use his connections to open a store at the front of the museum for people who didn' want to take the tour. This wound up being the museum's biggest revenue stream.

To turn things around, we needed a big draw. Stephen was a HUGE gamer. Like, HUGE! He actuall learned to read playing Legend of Zelda, and havin his mom help him understand the prompts. Additionally, retro video gaming was starting to become a trendy past time. Stephen and I proposed making a History of Video Game Console exhibit as our first cycling exhibit. It was a big stretch for James because he didn't play video games and didn't understand that part of nerd culture. But with our reassurance that this would be a great success, he agreed.

We spent the next two months getting everything together for this new exhibit.

Being the nerds that we were, we had the necessary connections to get every vintage console ever made for the exhibit. All we had to do was drive to Albuquerque, New Mexico to get them. We also had sourced a lot of amazing toys, posters, and more. I designed a whole Donkey Kong inspired timeline for guests to learn about each console's history, and we made plaques for each system filled with interesting facts.

I started sending out press releases, arranged for local media to come on opening day, and we held a press night for print media and local bloggers. With the building press and promotion, groups were booking tours in advance. We were on track for a textbook launch.

But what we didn't know was while we were in Albuquerque, the other assistant manager that James had hired, said that he thought the exhibit was going to be a big flop. He was not happy that Stephen and I had been brought back into the fold and that James had given us so much say-so over the success of the museum. This person planted seed after seed of mistrust and doubt into James.

The night before the exhibit was scheduled to launch, we went to James's house to get the key to the store for a 4am news segment the next day and he refused to give us the key. So much so that on the night before the exhibit was scheduled to launch, James unloaded his fears, concerns, and insecurities on us.

I was in total shock to the point of tears. James had asked us to come back, and we had done everything we promised and more. The museum was doing better than ever and on track for an amazing launch of their first exhibit. Why was he doing this?

Stephen was enraged!

The longer James stood there, venting about how he didn't think it would be this way, how he had expected something different, and how he just didn't get it, the angrier Stephen got. Finally, he snapped.

"We are out!"

He pulled out of the museum and canceled the exhibit in less than 60 seconds. I was stunned.

Innovation from Desperation

We had done so much work, gotten some amazing press coverage, tapped into so many connections, and were ready to make the museum grow. But it didn't matter. It all was going to be for nothing. Stephen and I were heartbroken.

You can't make someone understand or trust, even when you have earned it. It was *deja vu,* a total glitch in the Matrix. You really can't make someone do what is best for them, and sometimes, you just have to walk away.

MOMENT OF INNOVATION

I am not going to lie to you. These experiences cut me deeply. I cried, screamed, cried, just felt utterly defeated, and cried some more. I was truly hurt and took personally every wrongdoing against me. And how could I not! This was going to be my financial future, my new career, my shot at making a life on my own terms.

But as I lived through these experiences, it felt like 2007 again. I was getting rejected over and over for one reason or another. Why wasn't I good enough, and being treated like I didn't matter? Why would someone do this to me?

When I look back, I know I had to go through these

hardships. I needed to learn what to look for in a client or partner and to recognize the big red flags warning me about a potentially unhealthy business relationship. But I also really needed to learn what my time and talent were worth. I had to realize that not every opportunity is right for me, and I am not right for every potential client.

More importantly, I needed to learn that it is okay to walk away. I have a horrible habit of trying to please everyone, and it irks me when people don't like me. I mean, come on. I am awesome! Have you seen my gif library? In these situations, I found myself trying to do everything I could to make these horrible people happy and pleased with my work. It was almost like making excuses for an abuser and going back for more.

But in the end, I came out on top. These bad situations ended up being learning experiences for me, and great learning experiences for you, too. Those who hurt me genuinely missed out on working with someone who would truly love their brand and help them succeed.

That is why you need to know what you're worth and when to walk away. While it might sting to lose that client or opportunity, you are the winner in the end. The person that told you no or didn't see value in you and what you have to offer are the ones that missed out on someone pretty amazing.

And that "no" leaves room for the perfect "YES!"

What was one of the mistakes that taught you more than you wish it would have? Share it with me by tagging me @MrsDesireeRose with #shareyourinnovation on social media.

** Not his real name*

CHAPTER 4

FREE WORK AND STRATEGIC PARTNERSHIPS

While the mistakes I told you about in Chapter 3 are a big part of my business story, I also did a lot of things right.

I truly believe that anyone getting started in business needs to do two things:

- Take on free work (aka paying your dues)
- Make strategic partners (aka making friends)

I STILL do this in my business today. Whenever I am adding a new service or wanting to test something out, I always look for someone that I think I can achieve great success with. I then ask if I can do some free work on their behalf to figure out what works best for them and for what I am trying to accomplish.

When I was getting started with Pink Media, I did a lot of work for free. My big selling point was setting up Facebook Fan Pages for businesses. That service included creating Facebook Landing Pages and profile pictures that I called Social Media Business Cards.

The Social Media Business card came from earlier versions of Facebook. Back then, you could have a LONG profile photo and adjust the square profile picture to feature whatever you wanted in your news feed.

This became my signature service and how I planned to become a social media expert in my area. But first, I needed to find the right people to do some free work for and showcase my ideas. I never stopped networking, and I knew there were gems in my new and growing network. I was confident that I could offer this free service to them in exchange for their praise, accolades, and, hopefully, new business.

I first reached out to NetworkingPhoenix.com founder, Gelie Akhenblit, to ask if I could build these for her upcoming Facebook Fan Page. She and I had bumped into each other many times and had become friends. We were both working to make a name for ourselves through entrepreneurship, and she was helping the exact people I also wanted to do business with. I knew she was going to be a great strategic partner.

What my Social Media Business Cards looked like.

My work spoke for itself. Gelie loved what I made and praised it to her network. As a result of our partnership and her recommendations, I quickly started landing new business.

My next partnership was with a new leadership training program called Girlfriend University. I actually cold-called them, which to this day, I rarely do. I asked if I could provide them with my complimentary signature package in exchange for their online recommendation. They loved my work so much that they asked me to go through their weekend training. Of course, I did so and made some amazing connections with people I am still connected to today. This partnership not only allowed me to network with people I would never have had access to but also to get an amazing business development opportunity. All because I picked up the phone and gave value to someone.

One of the things I desperately needed help with was closing sales. I just believed that my hard work should speak for itself, and that should make people want to buy. This is SO not the case, and I knew I needed help. Then I met Linc Miller from Sandler Training. His coaching method was all about getting out of your comfort zone (and own way) to make things happen in your business. Of course, this training also came with a hefty price tag, so I figured why not pitch my services and see if we could exchange services, and he agreed. This was my introduction to the world of bartering. It also gave me the much-needed kick-in-the-pants to help me figure out how the hell to talk about my services in a way that would make people want to buy them.

Facebook Party

In my early networking days, I encountered a LOT of network marketing business women. It made so much sense because the economy had tanked, and people were looking for new ways to make money. Whether it was a side hustle or their full-time gig, network marketing was all the rage.

I went to so many networking events and met MLM (Multi-Level Marketers) people there. The companies and people were fine, and I found some that I really loved supporting. But no matter how great our relationship was, one thing kept happening over and over: they couldn't use my services.

Even if they were in a position to pay my fees, the company they represented had strict rules about what could be said or done online regarding their product. This was so frustrating to me, because this gigantic group of people made up 30 percent of the people I encountered on my business journey.

I was determined to figure out a way to do business with them in a way that they understood.

For those of you that may not know how most network marketing businesses work, the person interested in the MLM product partners with a distributor. You invite people that you know together to learn about the product. This is often done at one-on-one meetings or group events at your home. The distributor puts on a show and educates the people you brought. In return, you get a free gift based on the number of sales that are made. The more sales the distributor gets, the bigger your gift is.

As a social media marketer, I needed to use this same system. I needed to get distributors to bring their teams around social media, in some way. These would be people who love the distributor product so much they want to sell it, too.

And so was born Facebook Party!

A Facebook Party worked just like network marketing parties, but with a couple of twists. The distributor brought their team to their house, a coffee shop, or office room. Each team member paid $20 to learn about how to use Facebook for their business. As a reward, the distributor host got their business Facebook Page set up for free through the demo.

I taught these distributors all about Facebook. We covered everything from going over the interface, security, finding friends, and what to post. It was two hours of great information to help them expand their business. For me, it was another method I used to make money from this gigantic percentage of my networking community.

Attendees absolutely loved it! So many of them were totally confused about Facebook, how it worked, and why they should even bother. But this meeting allowed them to come together, learn, and grow their home business.

I did these for years, and every time, I received so much gratitude from those who came. When I would tell my fellow marketing peers about it, they would just facepalm about how easy and brilliant it was that I had found a way to play the MLM game with my rules.

This really taught me that sometimes you just have to find a way to adapt your business to help those around you. I was constantly meeting Network Marketers, and it just seemed like such a huge group of people to not do business with. They wanted what I had to offer. I just needed to find a scrappy way to get it to them.

MOMENT OF INNOVATION

Strategic partnerships don't always lead to immediate sales opportunities like it did with NetworkingPhoenix.com. But they can present you with unique and valuable experiences that you can use to move forward personally and professionally. This goes back to the "why not" mentality that led me to the current life I now lead. Opportunities are abundant and have more worth than you know. Not everything comes down to either dollars or nothing at all. Instead, it's about knowing what you are worth and the value you bring to a situation and a client.

I think it is also important that you be really specific about whom you do free work for and whom you partner with. You want to ask yourself a couple of things before going into any agreement with anyone:

- What value can I bring to them?
- What will I learn from this arrangement?
- What will I get from this relationship?
- What are the expectations of both parties?

When I made the free Facebook design work for

Gelie, I knew the value I would bring her was that she would have a well-designed and branded Facebook page. I learned about working with an established brand and the existing requirements they had in place like colors, fonts, and logo limitations. I also knew that she would promote my service to her network and also give me a recommendation. The expectations were that I would design her Facebook Business Card and Facebook Landing page, and in return, if she was happy with the final product, she would promote my service to her network.

If I wasn't able to clearly answer these questions, I would not have entered into the arrangement with her or anyone else. Just because it's free doesn't mean someone should walk all over you.

Same with making friends. Any friendship requires trust, a mutual agreement of expectations, humor, and zero judgment. Especially when you eat the whole pint of ice cream while wearing the same clothes you've been wearing for three days and you kind of smell.

Okay, maybe not EVERYONE is the last one, but you should know that hot mess is my default setting. (See, honesty!)

Make sure you know what you are getting yourself into. That starts with clear communication and management of expectations.

What was a project you did for free that turned out to be for your business? Tag me in a post about this moment @mrsdesireerose with #shareyourinnovation on social media.

CHAPTER 5
SOCIAL MEDIA DAY PHOENIX

My first year of business was such a weird jumble of awesomeness and hardship. But as I headed into my first anniversary of having my own business, I wanted to celebrate!

I had made the financial decision to become a member of my local Chamber of Commerce. With that came the opportunity to participate in a ribbon-cutting ceremony for my new business. This gave me some extra exposure and also some "let's celebrate Desiree" time. I wanted to rejoice in this moment with my family, along with the community that I was quickly becoming a part of.

Around the beginning of May, Meetup.com and Mashable began posting articles about Social Media Day (SMDay), just as they did in 2010. I had followed what other cities had done for SMDay, such as conducting meetups and learning sessions. Some communities even had their mayors declare June 30 as Social Media Day!

So, I thought I would do something crazy that I had never done before. I decided to put on an event in Phoenix. I was going to own Social Media Day in my community, although I had ZERO ideas how I was going to do it. But what did I have to lose?

The first thing I needed was to begin posting information on all the usual online places. So, I went to Meetup.com, claimed the Phoenix event, and put TBD (to be determined) in the spot where you would typically post location and description. I did know that June 30 was going to be the date for the event. I also set up a Facebook Page and a Twitter account under @SMDayPHX, leaving all the details blank except for the date.

I knew a couple of other things I wanted going into this: Strategic partnerships with brands that had a big social media following and could help me promote the event. I wanted it to be free, and I did not want to have to pay for anything. Keep in mind, I was still bootstrapping my business. The more than $400 I had paid to join the Chamber of Commerce was a HUGE deal to me financially, so I had limited financial resources for the SMDay event.

I started scrolling through Twitter, looking for a location that would be a good fit for the event. I needed a place that would be willing to partner with me for free. They had to have a big space with a bar so people could get drinks. There was one advantage to planning an event during the summer in Phoenix. Because of our desert climate, hotels, and other similar venues struggle with attendance. Our tourist season is October through April, and the June heat in Phoenix typically shuts people and businesses down. Most people head west to San Diego or north to Flagstaff to escape the heat. Because of this, businesses are looking for events to host.

I reached out to the downtown Phoenix Sheraton

Hotel. They had a solid social media presence and were open to new ideas. They also were wanting to get people into their wine bar during the week in the summer. I worked closely with the hotel's PR rep, who also handled the social media, because that was how it was done in the early days. With their help, I was able to use District American Kitchen and Wine Bar at the Sheraton as the location for the first SMDayPHX event.

With the location secured, it then became a matter of reaching out to brands, businesses, and individuals asking them if they wanted to be a sponsor in exchange for helping promote the event. I also asked for 500 free items from everyone interested in becoming a sponsor, so that I could make swag bags for the first 500 people that attended. I was clearly very ambitious, but I'll be damned because it worked!

The event began generating buzz online, and as the chatter grew, more and more brands reached out to ME, asking how they could be involved. Popchips not only gave us free chips but set up a Popchips bean bag lounge. Another local business, Snapbooth, offered to set up their booth so people could have a souvenir photo to take with them. US Airways Arena came to me and asked if they could donate 500 pairs of tickets to upcoming Phoenix Mercury (WNBA) games. Major League Baseball's Arizona Diamondbacks did the same for their upcoming 4th of July game.

I remember driving all over town, picking up the

donated items from the 25 businesses that partnered with me to help promote SMDay in Phoenix. I had to rope my friends and family into helping me stuff all 500 swag bags the weekend before the event.

I really wanted this event to be over the top great! While I worried that only 25 people would show up, I wanted to make June 30 Social Media Day in Phoenix and really solidify this day into our city's history. I wanted it officially proclaimed a "day," like all those other cities I was seeing online had done.

But apparently, in Arizona, cities can't proclaim official "days," only the governor's office can do that. Then, it becomes a statewide proclamation.

That is heavy, right?

With my mom's help and her ability to take my craziness and funnel it into official jargon, I applied to have June 30 proclaimed Social Media Day in the State of Arizona. In my application, I told them the purpose of my event was to use social media to bring people together and help support local businesses through this modern way of communicating. I marketed SMDayPHX to our state officials by saying, "Phoenix will join over 1,300 communities around the world, coming together to check-in, tweet, and update their Facebook status while connecting and engaging with each other and local business owners."

On June 15, I was out and about, doing something work-related when my mom called me.

"You got a big fancy envelope from the State of Arizona here!"

"NO. Freaking. WAY!"

She opened it and read, "Janice K. Brewer, Office of the Governor, proclaims June 30, 2011, as Social Media Day."

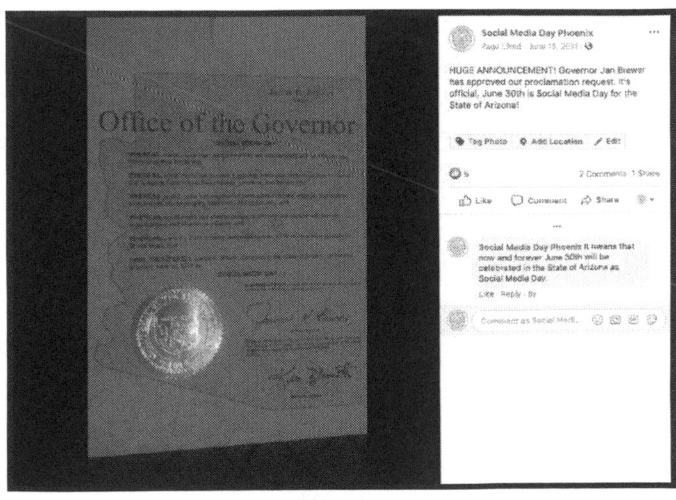

This was just amazing! Having this proclamation was a huge win and did so many things to catapult the event in many new ways. Because of the governor's proclamation, news about SMDayPHX was picked up by local media. It was also featured on Mashable internationally, and RSVPs for the event shot up!

Personally, the success of the event validated that I really was on the right track with my career. There had been just so many defeats, struggles, and being screwed over, but this felt like a stabilizing win. This proved to me that I was doing the right thing and that social media was growing and wasn't going away.

When June 30 came, I was overwhelmed by the amazing response! The line to register for the event was out the door. My awesome friends jumped in and started handing out name tags and swag bags while collecting email addresses. About an hour into the event, I got a chance to breathe and look around. The place was PACKED!

My contact from the hotel came up and hugged me because bar and food sales were off the charts. People were live tweeting, taking pictures, and telling others online how they loved the swag bags. It was a truly successful event, and I was just glowing with excitement.

On top of this amazing event, the icing on the cake for me came when my contact from US Airways handed me two box seat tickets to the Backstreet Boys & New Kids on the Block concert, which was literally starting at the end of the Social Media Day celebration. My best friend and I got to go celebrate the success of my event at an awesome concert!

I hosted Social Media Day commemorations for the next two years, handing it off to someone else when I left Phoenix for Air Force life. The subsequent two events I was involved in did not have the luster of the first one, mostly because the novelty about social media had worn off. They became ordinary gatherings with issues that needed to be solved and worked through, plus the need for a bigger marketing plan to compete with other events. In addition, there were literally cooler and more desirable places to go celebrate Social Media Day in June. Nearby cities like San Diego were able to attract big names to their events, plus they had the allure of cooler temperatures and nice beaches to lure Phoenicians.

Tyler Anderson
Social Media Day San Diego

Tyler Anderson is a social media marketing entrepreneur, speaker, and host of the Social Media Social Hour Podcast. He's the founder and CEO of Casual Fridays and is Executive Producer of Social Media Day San Diego. He has over 14 years of digital marketing, social media marketing, and public relations experience. He has worked with hundreds of brands on social media and content marketing initiatives.

As somebody who ran a social media marketing business, I, of course, was attuned to what Mashable and Meetup.com were doing with Social Media Day. When I went to see what Social Media Day event was happening in my local area, which was Phoenix at the time, I actually had no idea who Desiree was or who was behind it, but I saw that there was a Social Media Day Phoenix meetup at that swanky hotel restaurant bar in downtown Phoenix. So I RSVPed.

It was so cool!

It was like a giant networking party. Now, mind you, one, a big part of the success is because Desiree has done a great job getting businesses and sponsors involved. I'll always remember that photo booth that she had where people could take home actual fun pictures where they posed with fun social media props. And I remember the Popchips lounge that was there where people could lounge, socialize, and network. I think that was what made it successful first and foremost.

Then secondly, this also was still the early days of social media, so of course, everybody was like ... 'Oh my God! This is awesome!' Everybody was connecting on platforms like Twitter, checking in on Foursquare, and engaging with social media with each other live and in-person. Fast forward to today, I think we now just kind of chalk all that up as normal.

When my family moved back to San Diego shortly after that first Social Media Day Phoenix event, I knew there was a lot of potential in doing an event like this in San Diego. In 2012, I reached out to one client, Marriott Marquis, who was looking to do more with social media to build awareness. I knew that hosting Social Media Day San Diego would be a great way to make that happen.

I partnered with the guy who had claimed the Meetup page the previous year and basically used the Social Media Day Phoenix event as my inspiration. I got Popchips to be a part of the event and even got the day June 30th proclaimed a day for the City of San Diego, like Desiree did in Arizona.

It was a win all around because my client loved it, and it brought together many social media stars on the rise like Mari Smith, Amy Porterfield, and Michael Stelzner. We had a giant Twitter wall tracking all the engagement and posting the 900+ people who had attended were sharing.

Now Social Media Day San Diego is an annual event that brings the San Diego community together, and those seeking some fun in the sun to learn how to be better social media thought leaders and brands. But don't worry, that big fun networking party still happens, we just moved it to the beach.

MOMENT OF INNOVATION

I'll never forget a post I saw in 2010 "If your product or service sucks, social media won't fix it." Social media is not a silver bullet that's going to make any product successful. Just because you're going on social media doesn't mean you're going to sell a million widgets. If your product sucks, you're not going to sell a million widgets.

Just be a practitioner. Roll up your sleeves, get dirty. If you want to be an expert, you have to put in the time and fall in love with the process.

MOMENT OF INNOVATION

SMDayPHX was a huge success and confidence builder for me and taught me what I was capable of doing. I also learned not to be afraid of trying something new and thinking outside of the box.

To dominate and be a thought leader in whatever industry or niche you are in, you need to find a way to stand out, be bold, and let other people see you shine. An event is a great way to do that. It allows you to set the tone and pick the message, speakers, sponsors, and things. As the founder, creator, and overall authority, you are basically the benevolent overlord leading the people to your undeniable brilliance. (Too much? Eh - lol)

The one thing I can advise you on this matter is no matter what happens, put yourself on the stage as a thought leader. Give yourself prime stage time to share your genius, energize the crowd, and cement in their minds that you are the only possible expert on your subject. Only you can be their benevolent god - I mean, subject matter expert.

What are you an expert in? What makes you truly unique in your niche? Share it with me by tagging me @MrsDesireeRose with #shareyourinovation on social media.

CHAPTER 6

THE ENTREPRENEURIAL ROLLERCOASTER

The next few years of my business were a combination of steady growth and hard lessons. Still, those lessons went hand-in-hand with everything else I had going on in life.

The day after SMDayPHX, my boyfriend and I moved into an apartment in Tempe with our best friend. He was going to be attending Arizona State University (ASU) to get his Master's Degree. We needed a more affordable living option that did not have us living with our parents. As strange as it may seem, I got excited every month when I handed over my rent and bill money. That's because I was earning money from my own business. It was even more exciting when I had extra money left over to enjoy and to do things socially.

I knuckled down harder than ever by following up with all the businesses and individuals that attended SMDayPHX. I wanted to see who I could help by building out their social media strategy or managing their content. I kept attending three to five networking events a week and got to an excellent place by tripling my business that year. In the summer of 2012, I decided to get legit and rent office space because I was about to hire an employee and work with ASU on getting some interns.

I ended up finding office space for $400 a month, about 15 minutes away from my house. The one-room could fit four people, making it a tight fit, but cozy. I felt so fancy being able to walk in, say hi to the office assistant, and hold meetings in the common coworking conference room. I was actually becoming a boss and not just a social media professional. (High five to me!)

My Team

I had systemized my social media process, so it was easier to market and sell to businesses. Customers now knew exactly what they were getting each month. Any extra service they wanted would be provided at an additional charge. Since I had a system, I knew that I could easily train someone to implement it, so I put the word out in the social media universe that I was looking to hire a social media manager to join my team.

A friend of mine who was a local comedian applied for the job. She always did such a good job promoting herself and her gigs that I figured she would be a good (and hilarious) fit for the team. Once she was trained, she would be off to the races, and I could focus on sales and my new project of training interns.

Both my roommate and husband were students at ASU. They had mentioned that the school was always looking for businesses to participate in their internship program. I thought back to my college internship, and it gave me chills. It was horrible! I worked with a crime scene re-creation company once a week for 11 weeks to fulfill my credit requirement. The work included tasks such as scanning photos of horrific car accidents, and then putting them into 3D software for the team to reconstruct the scene for the forensic reenactment. I was bored out of my mind and would literally fall asleep waiting for work. I hated it and learned absolutely nothing.

But the internship I would offer would be totally different. It would be my chance to show these students what social media was really all about, give them value, and real-world experience.

Innovation from Desperation

I posted an internship opportunity on the ASU website and soon met Marc and Christine. Although they were from totally different backgrounds and on different career paths, we all instantly meshed. They eagerly jumped onto the Pink Media team, ready to learn about social media. They may have thought the job was going to be filled with taking pictures for hip companies or super fun, whimsical brands. But in reality, we were representing lawyers, roofers, and window companies.

I quickly showed them how to be social media marketers, and taught them to use the tools of the trade, BUT I also wanted to be sure they were learning what to do for their OWN brands. I felt that was important because establishing myself as a brand online was how I had been able to network and grow my business. I shared with them how the social media world works and how to cultivate a very specific brand of pure silliness and social media expertise. I didn't really veer off that course, remembering that I was sitting in a position of power, and what I said had influence. That is something I am still mindful of today.

My two interns were only six years younger than me but never knew a world without cellphones or the Internet. They weren't being taught social media responsibility in school. They had no idea that everything they posted online could haunt them forever. This mentality just wouldn't do for my "panda cubs."

So, off to the races we went.

When Marc and Christine weren't handling their small amount of real client work, I had them working on developing their personal brand. I made them dive deep into who they wanted to be, what jobs they hoped to pursue, and how they could become experts in their industry. By the end of the summer, they had developed their own blogs, established an online image, and had developed a plan for continuing to maintain that brand after their internship ended.

As a result of the positive feedback they had gotten from Marc and Christine, I wound up getting a call from ASU's prestigious Walter Cronkite School of Journalism and Mass Communication. The school was impressed by the work I had done with their interns and asked me to come to speak to their students about personal branding as part of an extracurricular workshop. They also kept feeding me interns to help one-on-one. It was one of my favorite opportunities, and all my former interns have gone off to do really amazing things with their online brands. I love continuing to follow them as they make their way into the world.

While all this was going on, my new social media manager was struggling. It seemed that no matter how much we worked together, she just wasn't getting the hang of the work. She confessed to me that she was even working after hours off the clock, trying to improve the social media content. I really wanted it to work out, but when one of my biggest clients threatened to leave, I had to fire her.

From this, I learned that no matter how well-intentioned someone is, some people have it, and some don't. Not everyone is cut out to manage social media. And that goes for any job or opportunity.

There are some businesses that I would be a bad fit for. Like restaurants. We are no good together. I can give them a strategy all day long, but at the end of the day, they need someone posting for them in the moment and taking pictures as situations arise. I can't do that for them. Why? Because I am not there. I can't plan ahead because it requires them to give me things that they don't seem to have time to give. You gotta know your strengths and weaknesses, and service-based businesses are my jam!

I remember working with a for-profit certification program called Training to You. They helped unemployed people get their certifications in tech-based skills. I worked with them to share their events online and create social media content based on the experiences that people using them were having. I even helped them launch their services to veterans when GI Bill 2.0 allowed service members to get tech certificates rather than pursue a college degree. Training to You would give me the information. I would turn around and put their messaging into small digestible posts that were actionable and converted prospects into new students.

Lean In To What You're Good At

The hardest thing I had to deal with was landing really great contracts, and just killing it for the clients, only to have them pull out without notice or advance warning. Once, I had a partnership with a local beauty blog. The client would offer an upgrade to her blogging and couponing services to include social media management done by our team. We would promote the salon, spa, events, or anything else she had going on to the salon's social media sites. Our monthly retainer with her added up to thousands of dollars. She and her customers loved what we were doing, until suddenly, and unexpectedly, she pulled the plug. She literally handed me a check for services rendered up to that point and stopped working with us.

For a small boutique business like mine, it was a serious pill to swallow. This was especially so because the salon owner ended up hiring one of her friends (who was doing all of her writing) to replace our team.

There were so many times when these big contract clients would be just cruising along doing great. Suddenly they would decide they wanted to have someone in-house manage their social media or turn it over to an intern. It made it hard for me because I would be losing work and income for the Pink Media team. Most often, it had nothing to do with the quality of our work, because we were doing a great job. They just decided to make a change.

When this happened, it made it difficult for my business to gain any solid financial footing, and I found myself begging for work. I also undervalued what I had to offer. It didn't matter that I was a trailblazer in social media, with a proven track record of success. My services were considered "disposable" by some, and I was expected to not take it personally.

After laying off my social media manager and watching my interns return to school, I gave up my office space and returned to working from home. I hired some independent contractors to handle the social media management tasks under my supervision. This allowed me to keep my overhead low and make it easier for me as clients came and went.

I started wondering, is this it for me?

Had my potential peaked?

Was managing small business accounts the most I was going to be able to do?

Was I ever going to get a chance to help a big business thrive on social media?

MOMENT OF INNOVATION

Even though my office time was short-lived, it was some of the best professional times I had. When you look at the entirety of my social media career, this time really taught me a lot and laid some solid foundations that stick with me to this day.

The biggest one is my love for helping others. I had the honor of working with six interns during those few years, each one more unique and capable than the last. We would have deep conversations and observations about what they wanted from their career and created a plan to help them get there. They are now doing things like running their own photography and video studios, traveling the world as digital nomads, and writing music and concert reviews for publications. I even hired one of them to be my videographer at my wedding!

And I got to be a part of their journey that helped put them on the path of success for the careers they wanted. This is something I still take time to do with people. I help them get focused on what they want from their life and brand then figure out what that path looks like. It really takes only a little time to show that you care about someone, and I personally feel that if you are capable, you are morally obligated to. Because that talk with you could be the difference between their success and failure.

This time also allowed me to get a taste of traditional work-life and discover that it is just NOT for me. As much as I love my team, I love that we can work when we want and how we want, with all the flexibility that working remotely offers.

As for losing clients, that is part of the game. And the best way to win that game is to never stop working your personal brand so that you can keep getting those leads.

I would encourage you to seek out an opportunity to mentor others, no matter where you are in life. You have experienced things and know things that others don't and that could really help them on their journey. You don't always need to have years of experience and be going gray; you just need to have a sympathetic ear and a desire to help. Heck, if the sixth graders at my kid's elementary school can mentor kindergartners, you can help someone too.

As for dealing with professional "setbacks" - that is just part of the business game. Whether it is taking a job purely for the experience and the paycheck (raises hand) or you try to be "professional" by having an office, these are all just roads on the drive of life. Sometimes you take detours or end up at a dead-end, but you don't stop trying to get to where you need to go. Like my favorite cartoon says "Take chances! Get messy! Make Mistakes!" (I think we can all agree that

Ms. Frizzle was the BEST mentor any of us could have ever asked for.)

What is your mentor situation these days? Are you mentoring anyone? Being mentored? Share that journey with me by tagging me @MrsDesireeRose with #momentofinnovation on social media.

CHAPTER 7
SOCIAL MEDIA PRODUCER

"We are letting you go."

I sat there, stunned. I was blank, wordless, and defeated.

How is this happening?

Again?

Really – over a tweet?

Okay, let's rewind the super dramatic beginning of

this chapter to give you some context.

At the end of 2012, I took a job at a computer repair company. Things with my freelance business were steady, but I needed extra money for my upcoming wedding. This job offered me an okay salary, benefits, and was just down the street from the townhouse where I lived with my fiancé and our best friend.

I knew what I was getting into since I was hired to basically be on call for marketing projects. But a couple months into the new job, I was bored out of my mind. I would go days without anything to do. I felt like that guy in Office Space, who did about 15 minutes of real work a week. Apparently, it was cheaper for them to hire someone full-time to flesh out the owner's ideas rather than work with a marketing firm to handle their projects.

So, I would go days and sometimes weeks without any real, time-consuming work. For some people, it would have been a dream. I had my own office and was left alone all the time. I would surf Facebook and the web, listen to audiobooks, take selfies of my OOTD (Outfit of the day), and work on my freelance business. But I am not most people. If someone is paying me for my time, I want to be busy doing something. I want to be useful, be a mover and shaker, make an impact, and be important.

Spanky

I would present them with ideas and proposals, just to be sent back to my office to sit and wait, because the owner definitely had serious ADD issues. Besides the steady pay, the silver lining to this job was I met Spanky. He was an energetic, creative director who I just loved spending time with. Spanky managed the company's podcast and did other things that I wasn't privy to. But he talked to me, which I LOVED! He would tell stories about this whole other life he had outside the office walls. He worked on amazingly creative projects for giant brands like M&Ms, ran a wedding photography studio, and was really focused on helping brands succeed through innovative marketing.

I remember asking him, "Why do you work here?! You could be doing 10 times more amazing things if you weren't stuck here all day!" He told me he had an illness that required a lot of medical care, and he needed the insurance that the company provided.

I then turned to him and said, "But you can get health care on your own. You don't need this place to handle that for you." This definitely stuck with him because, in a few months, he stopped working for that company and went out on his own. He called me after he put in his notice and told me that I had inspired him to make a move and go out on his own, because he wanted to be happy, create and do as he pleased, versus being stifled by a j.o.b. He is now a best-selling author, and owner of an amazing agency called Ad Zombies.

But when I had so sassily said to him that he didn't need this job for health insurance, he clapped back at me and said, "If you are so bored here, why not go where you can use your talents?"

And he was right!

The Hunt

I began looking for other jobs while at work. Yes, I know that was tacky, and I would NOT advise doing so, but I still did it. At that time, social media jobs did exist but were just starting to make their way into the everyday workplace.

After searching and searching, the perfect job popped up on my computer screen. CBS 5, the local network affiliate station in the Phoenix area, was looking for a Social Media Producer.

The job requirements were:

2-3 years of social media experience (check)
The ability to come up with creative sales ideas and

solutions to generate income from CBS 5's social media channels (check)

Train anchors and reporters how to use social media to build their personal reputations as well as to share CBS 5's news stories (check)

No news experience required (CHECK!)

I could do ALL these things. I was buzzing with ideas and excitement. If I was to describe my perfect job at that time, this was it!

I threw myself into researching and preparing for the interview. I would have to answer seven questions, and I wanted to better understand where they were coming from and why these questions were important. So, I did some reaching out.

I had recently connected with Lori, a former Social Media Producer at AZFamily, a rival station. I asked her about her struggles, victories, and interpretation of the questions. She said her biggest struggle was in constantly educating people from the newsroom to the salesroom to the boardroom about what social media REALLY was. It wasn't just another place to get numbers because, in the news business, numbers (ratings) are all that matters.

I also connected with my good friend, Denise, who was a producer for a morning lifestyle show on the local ABC affiliate. She explained to me how news works. She also bluntly told me that I was in for an uphill battle trying to educate a news organization about the difference between news and social media. It would be difficult to explain how they can work together while needing to be treated differently.

I felt ready. Between Lori, Denise, and Spanky, I knew how I was going to approach the written application and how I was going to answer their questions.

So, what were the questions? There were just seven, but they were a doozy to think through:

Of the following Social Media Platforms, which would you use and why, to grow the CBS 5 Social Media footprint: Facebook, Twitter, Pinterest, Tumblr, YouTube, Google+, MySpace, Instagram, or Social Bookmarking?

If you were asked to grow the CBS 5 Facebook likes to 60,000 by the end of the calendar year and to 100,000 by July 2014, what basic strategies would you adopt?

What strategies would you pursue to maintain high engagement on the CBS 5 Facebook Page?

How do you see the relationship between the CBS 5 Facebook page and CBS 5az.com?

What is your opinion of using contests to grow Facebook likes?

If you could create the ideal post for the CBS 5 Facebook page, what would that be? Please draft an example.

What tactics would you employ to improve and increase CBS 5's SEO ranking?

These aren't bad questions, but they miss the point regarding what social media is all about. Everything in the questions was about numbers (just as Lori had said), and I knew that I would need to drastically re-educate them and be as honest as I could.

My Response to No. 2

This is hard for me to answer because I know the answer you want to hear. I understand from a corporate level that they see success as the number of Likes and Followers versus the reporting, which shows social reach, klout score, variability, and growth. I could easily say, "Yes! That is so easy because I am SO amazing" then go buy Likes by the thousands. But that is only going to hurt the station.

But there is also a fundamental mindset change that needs to be made: Likes don't equal leads. If we want the station to have a valuable social network, we need to be focused first and foremost on engaging content.

Recently, I sat down with my friend Lori, a former social media producer for AZFamily.com. She told me a great anecdote about how a follower was wanting to watch a live story on the website, but the feed wasn't working. She turned to Twitter to tell AZFamily so they could fix it. They continued to have an on-going conversation about what was happening so she could be in the loop. Clearly, this woman trusted AZFamily for her news but didn't watch them on TV, only on social media. She got everything she needed from Twitter, Facebook, and the AZFamily website. THAT relationship, THAT connection, THAT engagement should be the goal for all stations. Because that woman will now always turn to AZFamily as a trusted news source. We need to be that trusted source for all the others like her.

If you look at ABC 15's Facebook page, yes, they have 100k+ Likes on their page. But if you look at their engagement ratio of Likes to viralbility, it is minuscule. They pushed so hard to grow their following by doing iPad give away after iPad give away, that they aren't building a valuable, focused audience.

They are just collecting a following of cheapskates that want free things.

Now that being said, I think it is entirely doable to build a growing, valuable following for CBS 5. I think setting goals for engagement, posts, and viralbility will be more measurable and financially sound than "Likes" goals. We can take an engaging audience to the bank through marketing and sales opportunities and non-traditional revenue streams.

Some examples of how we can grow an engaging audience are:

Community driven contests: A great sales option will be turning to companies in the Valley looking to increase their following by cross-promoting with us. We will be able to sell them a contest, news spot, and daily promotion from the station for the contest.

Our reporters: Our reporters are a group of individual brands connecting with people in a personal way that will always be different than the station. For simple reasons like "I just their face," or "I like how they report." We need to be able to empower and train them on how to use these tools effectively. They can do this by telling the story, sharing in the experience, and cross-promoting to the station. By empowering them through building their own brand, they will be more likely to do this because it will be theirs, but the station will be benefiting.

Following and reporting the trends: it is important to be looking for the next big story. It will be the responsibility of the social media team and the station to use social media to find those stories.

After applying, I heard back in just a couple days to set up an interview. While the atmosphere for the interview was casual, the process was intense. The station had never hired someone for this job, nor did the position exist anywhere in the Meredith Corporation, the publicly traded company that owned the station. This position was as a producer, which would have me on the newsroom floor, under the direction of the Creative Department. So, I was interviewing with the Director of Creative Services and the person in charge of design.

After that was a panel interview with the Station Manager, News Manager, and the Director of Creative

Services. I wore a bright red dress that was professional but powerful and filled me with confidence. I had ZERO intention of walking away from the station without that job.

After candidly and accurately answering all the panel's questions, the Creative Director and Design Director took me to lunch. Over lunch was where I made my last pitch for the job.

I laid out my 60-day plan. It was an in-depth strategy based on extensive research on all the different people and channels that CBS 5 had at their disposal. This plan included how I would integrate into CBS 5, what areas I would tackle and when, and what training needed to be done. I also covered what the branding should look like, how to add sales into the social media mix, and my plan for growth on all platforms. I had printed out my plan for them, and over salads, I broke down each part, step-by-step, answering, and asking questions along the way.

By now, I knew that news people love numbers. So, as icing on the cake, I presented them with a side-by-side numbers comparison provided by Scoreboard Social. That was a competitive social media analytics tool my friend Tyler had created. This report compared Like numbers, brand engagement percentages, number of posts, and daily post engagement percentages. It also had a fun option where you could see the top five posts from each page.

SCOREBOARD SOCIAL

Weekly Competitive Report
02/16/2013 - 02/22/2013

www.scoreboardsocial.com
858.707.5467

Facebook

Page	Total Likes	Were Here	People Talking About This	Brand Engagement	Posts	Daily Post Engagement
KPHO CBS 5 News	27,009	Not applicable	7,444	27.56 %	58	9.69 %
Fox 10 - KSAZ-TV	39,626	Not applicable	10,520	26.56 %	145	15.00 %
12 News	51,317	Not applicable	8,473	16.51 %	54	8.49 %
ABC15 Arizona	107,292	0	15,662	14.60 %	45	10.44 %
3TV Phoenix	26,748	0	1,579	5.90 %	28	2.00 %

Being able to present my 60-day plan and show them by the numbers where they were and how they could improve impressed them. They could easily know what to expect from me and how I would measure our growth.

The next day they called and offered me the job.

Press Pass

I happily signed the paperwork, gave my notice at the computer repair company, and started to prepare for this new phase in my professional career. I finally had a job where I was wanted, where I could make an impact, and use my creative talents. It was thought-provoking, the company was big, so there was no fear of losing my job due to downsizing. I also thought since it was a new and innovative position, there was room for error and growth.

True to form, nothing is official until it is posted on Facebook. So, after finishing with HR, getting the tour of the Newsroom, participating in my first meeting, and getting a desk, I was handed my badge. I proudly posted an update and changed my profile picture.

I spent my first few weeks meeting with reporters, answering questions, and training them on what to say and how to manage their personal brands. I talked with the News Director about what she needed from me and how I could support her by bringing her trending topics from the Internet. I gave them suggestions and strategies for how we could integrate social media into their news broadcasts.

I started managing news stories and putting together a steady system for sharing these stories online. I had been told repeatedly that the website was one of the biggest revenue streams for the station, and was single-handedly paying my salary. I was able to work with the Web team to figure out a system for sharing breaking news so that we could post it in tandem with a link to the website.

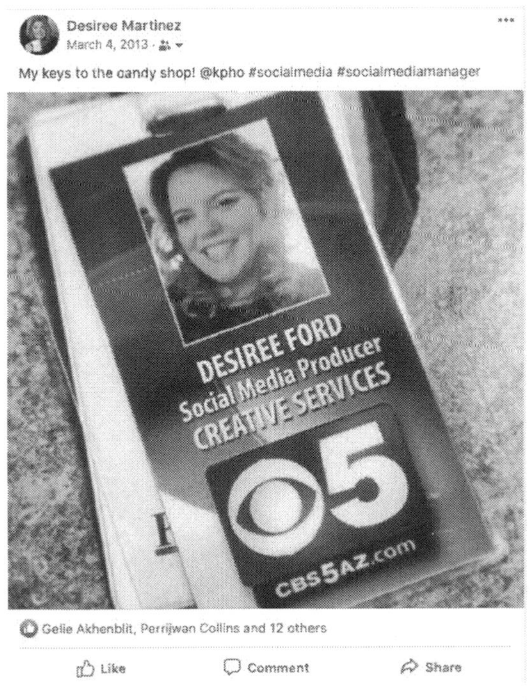

I was even able to parlay one relationship into a fun social media and news collaboration segment. Phoenix is known for giant dust storms during the summer monsoon season. They roll into town and when photographed just right, look like they are going to eat the city. But besides being really dangerous to drive in, they make a horrible mess.

One of my friends was the Marketing Director for a local car wash. We had a great idea to give away free car washes to anyone who posted a picture of their dirty, dusty car on the CBS 5 Facebook page. I took pictures of my own dirty car. Then, the morning and noon news teams promoted this special event on air with the image of my vehicle, including the words "Wash Me" written on the back window. I even got to take the CBS 5 News van to the car wash to get it washed and do social media posts.

We got hundreds of photos, and the car wash posting got thousands of visits during those 48-hours. It was a fantastic and successful event for the station, our Facebook page, and the car wash.

Numbers

While all this was great, it wasn't all smooth sailing.

Daily, I was being asked what our Facebook Like numbers were and what contests we could do to get more Likes. It was made clear to me shortly after starting that I had to answer to the "old white guys" on the board at Meredith with Like numbers. Even though I was right about engagement and the purpose of social media, they didn't care. All that mattered was having more Likes than Fox 10 down the street.

The Fox affiliate was the top-ranked station in Phoenix across the board. They had fun personalities, did risky news, told cutting edge stories, and had started giving away TVs for Likes during their morning show. I had to come up with a solution to compete with them.

Every quarter CBS 5 would do a charitable contribution and story series. The quarter I started working there, the charity was a local food pantry that helped area families. My idea was to do a Like contest where for every Like on the CBS 5 website, we would give one dollar to the charity. In reality, CBS 5 was going to donate $3,000 no matter what, but being able to tie it to a social media campaign was an added bonus. We promoted the Like contest on Facebook and Twitter, and the news anchors mentioned it during the 5:00 a.m., 12 noon, 7:00 p.m., and 10:00 p.m. newscasts.

Well, we got the 3,000 Likes, but it was harder than I expected. I had figured people would gladly Like for a good cause. But while most people were up for it, just as many people ignored it. Some left bad comments, such as, "you should donate no matter what!"

It was a hard lesson to learn, but if it comes down to winning an iPad or TV versus helping a charity, people will always pick the iPad or TV. It is the epitome of "What's in it for me?"

Another struggle I ran into was a lack of innovation. One day our lead sales person came to me saying Qwest was rebranding as CenturyLink. They were looking for a new project to sponsor that was aligned with their vision of high-speed internet and cutting-edge technology. At the time, Google+ was starting to take off. With hundreds of millions of users trying out this new social network from the biggest search engine on the planet, it was prime time for an innovative idea.

I had suggested doing a short five-to-ten minute daily or weekly feature with the station's beloved morning weatherman, about the best things to do in Phoenix. It could be about new local restaurants, events, shows, or anything else so long as it had to do with things to do in Phoenix. It could be done for Google+ and sponsored by CenturyLink, who was willing to put up $100,000 to start with for what they saw as a good idea.

The idea was shot down over the lack of control over pre-roll ads and because Google+ was too new, management wasn't willing to experiment. This shouldn't have been a surprise since I had started getting more and more push back, the longer I worked there. It wasn't just a couple big things, but a lot of small things that were causing struggle after struggle, making it harder and harder to do the job I was hired for.

The Tweet

On Monday, April 15, 2013, the Boston Marathon bombing happened at the finish line of the historic race. It was a horrible terrorist attack on America, resulting in three deaths and hundreds of injuries, including 16 people who lost limbs. CBS 5 actually had a producer who was running in the race.

Experiencing that on the newsroom floor was a unique experience. Not only was everyone waiting to hear that our producer was okay, but they were calling anyone they could think of to get a lead. The News Manager was yelling orders to reporters and calling meetings, then booking flights to neighboring airports so they could have "boots on the ground" in Boston. Of course, footage of the bomb going off kept re-airing, and the steadfast but somber reporters were there to comfort viewers.

All week, it was a constant cycle of hurry up and wait. Whenever any report or piece of news came on, we were ready to update the website and social media. We all had television monitors at our desks, and we watched the coverage and talked about it among ourselves. When our producer returned from Boston, she told us the police asked for her iPad and phone. They hoped to gather any photos she had from the event that might help them piece together what happened.

Thanks to all the smartphone and tablet footage, the country was given the names and shown the faces of two suspects, the brothers Dzhokhar and Tamerlan Tsarnaev, and the manhunt was underway.

Innovation from Desperation

On Friday, April 19th, the manhunt reached an unprecedented height when thousands of law enforcement officers searched a 20-block area of Watertown, Massachusetts, resulting in the shootout and, ultimately, capturing Dzhokhar. You probably remember seeing the video of him hiding under a boat tarp and surrendering to the police. The other brother, Tamerlan, was briefly captured but died at the scene after being shot and run over, allegedly by his brother.

I remember throughout the conflict, standing at the circular workstation in the middle of the newsroom with the evening News Producer and one of the Website writers listening to the police scanner. It was intense, and then the officers started shouting, "We caught him! We caught him! WE CAUGHT HIM!"

There was so much relief, but we also all had a job to do. I walked back to my desk, pulled up Twitter, and sent out a tweet saying, "The Boston Bombers have been caught by Massachusetts Police! www.CBS 5az.com." I was so happy to write that tweet and to be able to end the week delivering such happy news to the people of Phoenix.

Within a couple of minutes, one of the News Manager came storming out of her office screaming, "WHO SENT THE TWEET ABOUT THE BOSTON BOMBER BEING CAUGHT?" I was really taken aback by her anger, but since I had sent it, I told her I did. She didn't hear me, probably because I wasn't really shouting back that I had done it, mostly out of shock and fear.

She screamed again, "WHO SENT THE TWEET ABOUT THE BOSTON BOMBER BEING CAUGHT?" This time louder, and with my hand raised, I said, "I did!" She ordered me to delete it, and then stormed out of the newsroom. Within a couple of minutes, my phone rang.

It was my boss.

"You need to come to my office."

I knew what was about to happen. I walked out of the newsroom, knowing I would never see it again.

Thankfully, the News Manager wasn't there, but my boss was clearly distraught. He turned to me and said, "We don't report news based on police scanner information. We also have a very strict code when it comes to reporting news that it must be vetted through multiple sources before we talk about it. Now, it has been confirmed that Boston Bombers were caught, so you got lucky. But the News Manager wants you fired."

Wasn't this the company that wanted me to grow with them, I thought? Didn't they say "they would train me" with all I needed to know about the news? How is there not any room for human error?

I sat there, stunned and speechless. I said nothing.

My boss told me to go collect my things and that I was going to be suspended while he and the powers that be figured out what to do. I spent a week just waiting. I then received an email with a time to come in. I was taken back to his office, where I saw a box containing all my belongings.

"We are letting you go," he said. "I tried to fight for you, but this is just something that we can't get past."

I didn't say anything. I just nodded while tears ran down my face. I handed him my badge, grabbed my box, and walked out.

Processing

When I reflect on what happened, I feel that whoever got that job next was probably going to meet the same fate I did. It was too new of a position with a lot of barriers to break through. I remember seeing the job posted about two months after I was fired. The first item on the requirement list was "news experience."

I remember after getting CBS 5 more than 3,000 new Likes, it wasn't good enough for them, so they asked me what superficial contest we could run to get Likes. I gave a giant sigh and jokingly said, "Why not offer to pay someone's rent or mortgage for a year!" My boss's eyes lit up, and he said, "We have the budget; we can totally do that!" I was dumbfounded. A month after I was gone from CBS 5, they ran that contest, getting them their 60,000+ Likes.

There is a lot to unpack from my experience at CBS 5. I think the biggest takeaway in regards to social media is social media hasn't changed. It is still about building valuable and trusting relationships, not about the number of Likes. Many people STILL get caught up in vanity metrics like how many Likes or followers someone has or what their sub count is.

What matters most are the relationships that you have with your audience. The questions around numbers should be "What are your engagement numbers?" or "How many views do you have?" Or "How many clicks and conversations do you get from your posts?" These are the measurable things that matter when it comes to social media numbers.

While $100,000 might be a drop in the bucket for a company like CBS 5 and Meredith Corporation, it would have given them the money to test a new idea. They could have experimented with seeing if they could generate more income in different ways. Such as getting special events or products to pay to be featured as they do on the morning shows. But because they didn't understand it, it was turned down.

Innovation from Desperation

When it comes to social media, short-sightedness is just going to make it harder and harder to keep up. At the time I'm writing this book, Gary Vaynerchuk (Gary Vee) is telling everyone to get on TikTok because that is where the kids are. "You need to figure out how to be there because if you wait, something will be out that will have everyone's attention," he says.

Even after ten years of being a social media professional, I still meet business owners who say they don't have a Facebook Business Page. Some of them don't even have personal accounts. It is too hard for them to figure out, they don't have time, or they tried it once, and they didn't get sales. These are people who aren't thinking ahead, not being innovative, and just don't understand what social media is all about.

If these kinds of people don't undergo a mind shift, they won't be able to stay in business. In 2015, CBS 5 and AZFamily 3 merged, resulting in dozens of lost jobs, and cross country moves to new markets for some staff members. It also left a very confused viewing audience. This happens when companies don't innovate. They get gobbled up by those who do to cut costs for someone else's bottom line.

Getting fired might have been a blessing because AZFamily 3 was leading the way in social media for their station and the news community. I might have just lost my job anyway two years later during the merger.

MOMENT OF INNOVATION

The lesson to learn is this: Trying to convince people who just don't understand is also going to be frustrating, and those are not people you want to work with. While there is something to be said for taking on a challenge, it often comes at the cost of your personal and professional sanity and ethics.

If you walk away with anything from my intense experience, I hope it is that you remember what social media is and always will be. It is a place to connect and build relationships with people. That shouldn't come at the expense of trying new things, even if they might fail.

Have you ever been fired from or lost an amazing opportunity? What did you learn from it? How did you overcome it? I know it might be hard to share, but please tell me how you overcame this hardship by tagging me @MrsDesireeRose with #shareyourinnovation on social media.

CHAPTER 8
MARRIAGE, MILITARY AND MOTHERHOOD

After losing my job at CBS 5, things in my life just seemed "blah." I had planned to build my whole life around this job and basically ride-or-die with them for the foreseeable future. Now what was I going to do?

I had to do some scrambling to find a new place to live since I had given up my lease to live closer to the station, and was no longer going to be able to afford the new place. Also, I had to bring all the work I had a team of contractors doing back in-house because that was going to be my new income.

After the shock of losing yet another job wore off, my fiancé and I had to figure out what to do next. How were we going to make money? Where were we going to live and how could we support a family? These nagging questions weighed on our minds all of the time. We finally had a really candid and action-driven conversation about our next steps. We decided it was time to investigate every option and opportunity.

I began looking at social media jobs all over the country, and searching for more business opportunities. I even started pricing vans or a small RV to buy, live, and travel in. Stephen began looking for a summer job because he was still in college, and even went and talked with an Air Force recruiter.

We looked at option after option, but doors kept slamming shut. I would interview for job after job, but nothing worked out. I had enough client work to support us financially, and pay for our pending wedding. Other than that, nothing exciting was happening. And getting an RV or a van was not feasible financially, so we couldn't make that happen.

Marriage

We were abruptly distracted when my soon-to-be in-laws came to us at the end of July. They said they were going to be moving to Guam for a job and wouldn't be able to make it to our planned October wedding. They asked us if we would consider moving the wedding up dramatically to August 13th. That was just TWO WEEKS away!

If it had been any other family member, we would have said no, but when the mother of the groom asks to see her only son and last child get married, you make concessions. So, off to the races we went and pulled off an amazing and memorable Mario Kart themed wedding (seriously, an elegant shabby chic Mario Kart themed wedding). I only wish that the friends and family who weren't able to come could have been there.

Google Glass

At the beginning of 2013, Google introduced the world to Google Glass. Google Glass, also known simply as "Glass," were smart glasses designed to let users have a virtual experience. With them, you could ask questions, take pictures and videos, get directions, and more with the device you wore on your face like a pair of glasses.

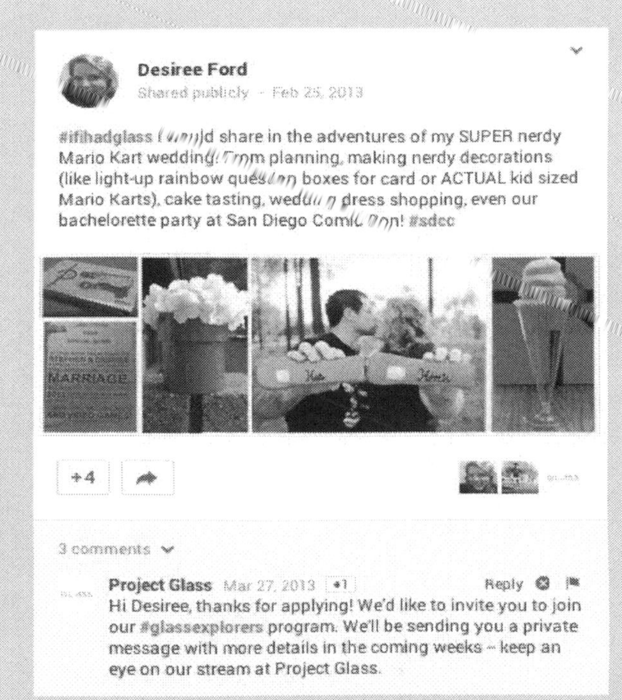

To help test and market their new product, Google launched an online campaign on Twitter and Google+ called #IfIhadGlass. People could enter to become a Beta tester based on what they would do if they had Google Glass.ot one to miss an opportunity, I posted on Google+ that I would use Glass to share the adventures surrounding my wedding planning. They selected me to join the #GlassExplorer program! I had 14 days from the time I was chosen to join the program and pick up the device.

Now keep in mind I had JUST lost my job, and Google wasn't just giving these bad boys away. They came with a $1,600 price tag, and I had to travel to one of three Google locations to pick them up. I was not about to miss out on this once-in-a-lifetime opportunity that could really help my business, so I got creative.

I emailed every one of my clients offering discounted work if they would pay me in advance to help me raise the money to get Glass. And it worked! I raised $1,500 in 48 hours, claimed my Google Glass, and booked a time to head to the Google offices in Venice Beach, California.

Having Glass opened up some amazing opportunities for free press and media spots. Also, I earned a lot of credibility in the marketing world because I had used social media to get this new tech device. I was even able to let my Google Glass be used on a model in a show for Phoenix Fashion Week. An article about it was also written talking about the merger of tech and fashion.

Sad to say that Google soon shut down Glass because it was clunky and awkward, but I did get to use it at my wedding. I had one of my interns attend to be my social media correspondent for my friends and family. She posted pictures and updates and wore my Google Glass during the ceremony.

When we came back from our Disney World honeymoon, things got really crazy. Before our wedding, I had locked in an amazing opportunity with a local marketing agency. I was going to help them manage the social media creativity for the upcoming Show Your Disney Side campaign, which was going live in a few months. It was the PERFECT opportunity for me because it combined my obsession with Disney with my love of creating great social media content.

Military

Upon returning to reality after the honeymoon, I started the contract opportunity only to find out I was pregnant (thanks, Disney magic!). As if that life-changing news wasn't enough, Stephen got a call from the Air Force recruiter he had talked with that summer.

There was an opening for him.

At this point, we were just overwhelmed with all that life was throwing at us. We were newlyweds and about to become parents. We were living in a 600-square-foot one-bedroom apartment and had no health insurance. Everything about our financial future was up in the air.

We also wanted to experience normal things, like traveling and being good parents. We were really sick of the grind that entrepreneurship and the job market kept putting us through. For me, it was a constant state of highs and lows, chasing people down for money, crazy hours, and a lot of work. As soon-to-be parents, this was not the lifestyle we thought was going to be right for us.

Military life was looking more and more like a nice, stable and reliable option. So, we took the plunge, and on November 12th, I kissed my husband goodbye as he headed to San Antonio, Texas, for basic training.

During that time, I began working on my exit strategy from Pink Media. Stephen and I had decided that I was going to become a stay-at-home-mom. We both had grown-up as latchkey military kids, and our moms worked way too hard and way too much. We decided that I would stop seeking new clients but keep servicing the ones I had, and just let the business naturally fade away.

After basic training, we moved to our first duty station at Dyess Air Force Base, near Abilene, Texas. I was almost 36-weeks pregnant, which was not ideal for a move, but since when does anything in military life go as planned? It was a whirlwind move. We had so much to do to get settled before our baby came. We were getting adjusted, finding a house on base, unpacking, setting up the nursery, and figuring out what military life was going to be like for us. Meanwhile, I had to make sure the clients I was still managing were going to be okay once I had our baby.

Innovation from Desperation

There were two interesting aspects of the decision to step away from my business. First, was how easy it was to do (especially since I moved away from my network). Second, was the weird feeling that social media was moving on without me. So many things had changed in social media while I was trying to figure out how to keep my husband and me alive. While I was waddling around pregnant, trying to keep up with the routines of eat, poop, and sleep, social networks like Tumblr and Pinterest were taking off in popularity. Snapchat had become the new kid on the block, and brands were increasingly embracing social media. They were learning that social media was the way people preferred to communicate with brands, especially when it came to customer service.

While I was obsessively taking pictures and videos of my son's every move, the social media universe was starting to see amazing success. Social events, such as the ALS Ice Bucket Challenge (where people dumped buckets of ice water on their heads) began springing up. They were used to bring awareness of specific diseases and causes and to encourage donations. Live streaming also started to gain serious traction with apps like Periscope and Meerkat (RIP). Facebook added live streaming to its platform in 2016, and it is still going strong today.

Vincenzo Landino - Fireball & Meerkat

Vincenzo Landino is a first-generation Italian-American and third-generation entrepreneur who is the CEO and co-founder of The Landino Group, a modern-day media parent company, holding the following: Aftermarq, a video production studio; Brainwork Media, a podcast production and network; and Landino PR, a new age public relations firm.

I was marketing for some small and medium-sized regional companies. I reached a point where I was like, "All right, I'm done. I don't want to work for anybody. I don't even want to be side hustling anymore. I just want to reach an income beyond what I am getting now." I had cut off that corporate paycheck and jumped onto doing social media marketing.

When it comes to social media from the beginning, I always treated it like a place to grow a brand or a business. I had looked at social as an opportunity for small businesses to make connections and money with these tools where other people thought, "oh this is just a place for kids." And in my stubbornness, I just wanted to prove people wrong. I wanted to show them that it was possible to make money with social media, even if I didn't know how to do it.

Fast-forward to Meerkat coming out, I was behind-the-scenes tweeting, managing social networks for brands and doing my thing, but people don't actually know you. I was just another avatar on the screen that people didn't have a close personal connection to. So, when Meerkat came out, I was like, "Man, there's a social aspect to video that makes it so much more appealing." The fact that you could communicate in real time, and answer their questions, you call them out by name, it was just perfect. My family members used to say, "the sweetest thing a person can hear is their own name," and that just stuck with me.

Meerkat was just PERFECT! People could see my face, hear my tone and passion, and I could really shine in real-time. I remember once I got stood up for a date and decided to go live for a stupid amount of time singing songs while drinking. People would come in and out and make requests, including Gary

Vaynerchuck, which has since evolved into a personal relationship. This really woke me up and showed me that I could reach out and touch people, that I could have never had the opportunity to, if it weren't for hitting that live button and doing something I was interested in.

It revealed to me that people want to see YOU as a person and Meerkat, well, live stream video in general, allowed me to do that.

So many amazing opportunities and craziness ensued over the years with random shows, Christmas karaoke, and Twitter conversation hosting (which was how I met my wife). I even started hosting live content for big brands like Applebee's and Barilla Pasta.

It was a huge eye-opener for me and gave me the opportunity to really work through the foundational needs of video and live streaming for brands. So when social networks like Blab and Meerkat shut down, because Facebook and Periscope were too big, the foundation of what to do and how to "perform" didn't change. It's always about showing up, giving value, and being yourself. So much of live streaming has changed, and the expectations have changed, but it is always interesting to think back to those early days on Meerkat and how raw and real they were.

MOMENT OF INNOVATION

You've just got to go for it. You got to go for it. I hate to echo some other folks' taglines and stuff, but sometimes you have to push the button. Sometimes you have to write that blog post; you have to look stupid on an Instagram story. Not even sometimes, you have to do things that others are going to think, "Oh, that's stupid. That's dumb, what an idiot," like you have to.

If I hadn't done that first stream on Meerkat, my life would have turned out so different. It comes down to those moments. If you don't take the chance to see if that opportunity could change or define your life.

Motherhood

All this social media life was going on around me, but I couldn't have cared less. My son and being a mom were my new obsessions. I loved it so much and thought I was such an "expert" that I launched a mommy blog called "My Mom's Geeky." I shared nerdy mommy craft projects for kids like making ninja turtle beanies, or making your own Batman Cart cover. I also posted recipes and product reviews. It was a lot of fun.

But when I got pregnant with my daughter in February of 2015, things changed. On top of being constantly exhausted, I also started to feel purposeless. Trying to be the best mom I could be was beginning to get me down. I felt like all I did was take care of my son, the house, the dogs, and my husband. There wasn't anyone taking care of me.

Now, if there is one thing I am good at, it is self-care. I have NEVER been one of those moms with damaged clothes, everything unkempt, or going crazy from lack of me-time. My husband and I both know that I need sleep, and regularly scheduled meals to do what needs to get done.

An important part of my self-care lies in having a purpose. Being a mom to me isn't a purpose, but a part of my life. I know countless mothers who are absolutely amazing and find happiness, fulfillment, and meaning from motherhood. But for me, it was starting to feel like a j.o.b., and one that wasn't giving me j.o.y. Don't get me wrong, I love my kids, and I will always be their biggest cheerleader and supporter. I love sharing my life with them because they are my why, but they don't fulfill my mental health needs.

So, how does a military spouse who is three months pregnant, and has a 12-month old who just learned how to run, fix this problem? Turn to Facebook, of course.

One of the most amazing things about social media is how it keeps people connected, and I mean EVERYONE. With Facebook, my family and friends could stay in the loop about what was going on in our lives. Facebook has been an amazing way to follow the growth of my kids and our family. And, it has the added benefit of being a digital archive of all our adventures and milestones. You may have had the same experience.

When we got our orders to Dyess, I immediately went to Facebook to see what I could learn about this new place we would call home. I discovered there was a Dyess Spouses Facebook Group. It's a fun fact that every military station around the world now has a spouse's group. There, incoming families can get the lowdown on what they need to know about the area. They can ask questions, connect, share, socialize, and vent. It makes transitioning to a new duty station SO much easier than in the days before the Internet and social media.

Desiree Martinez

The Dyess Spouses Group became a way for me to see what was going on in my area and quench my need for purpose and fulfillment. I discovered MOPS (Mothers of Preschoolers), local playdates, and witnessed my fair share of drama. I saw a LOT of people complaining about work. Working when you are the spouse of someone in the military can be a challenge!

The sad fact is that one in four (24-percent) of military spouses is unemployed. The number who are underemployed is more than half (55-percent). Military families are constantly moving, making it difficult to build a strong resume. In the military, the mission always comes first for everyone in the family, not just the service member. So, when Uncle Sam says jump, everyone in the family is affected and forced to make adjustments. Child care is costly, and for a young military family, it can cost so much to put your child into daycare that it makes no financial sense to work at an entry-level job. Because of that, most military spouses are forced to find a side hustle. The most common one is network marketing, which can be lucrative if you can work it right, and give it the time and attention it takes. But it also takes time and often a start-up investment, when military spouses typically need money now.

The financial stress causes many psychological issues for military spouses too, because they want to financially contribute to their family income. Doing so allows them to live comfortably versus paycheck-to-paycheck. The financial stress causes a lot of damage to relationships because when one person makes all the money, it can lead to power struggles and worthlessness. I personally witnessed physical and psychological abuse among military families because the service member was using the money, the military, and their living situation as a tool to control their spouse. The spouse would have to beg for things like new clothes for themselves or to do something fun. It typically ended up a mess.

This sad reality also caused me to flashback to my childhood. I remembered back in 1991, our Marine Corp family moved from Orange County, California to Okinawa, Japan. I was almost six, and my parents were 25. My dad was an E-5, and my mom was a secretary with serious waitressing skills. She had no problem getting work in California, but Okinawa had some limitations, as you might expect. My mom looked for work for months and couldn't find anything except house cleaning and random odd jobs. So, she and my dad agreed she would go back to the States, live with family friends, and work to add income to our family. More than 25 years later, I saw that employment was still an issue for military spouses.

Everything about this situation bothered me so much that I knew I needed to do something. I am a fixer. It is just what I do. Don't come to me spilling your guts and expect me to pat you on the back saying, "there, there, it will be okay." I am going to give you the truth, options, and a game plan for solutions.

I was going to help, which would give me purpose and fulfillment. It would allow me to contribute to my military spouse community in an unexpected way.

MOMENT OF INNOVATION

Life am I right!?

Some days I feel like it is just me that is living at a crazy mock 15 pace, but honestly that is all I know. I am just one of those people that hates still. Like taking me camping is a nightmare. There is only so much stargazing and smore eating I can do before irritation and boredom sets in.

But whatever your pace is, it is important to be self aware and adaptable. Being able to know your limitations, strengths, and what you can and can't do is going to be what give you success in all that you do.

I think it is also important to note, that when you get off your destined path, life still continues without you. The innovation train doesn't just stop because you decide to get off. And what is worse is that it can be hard to get back on it again. This is why older people tend to struggle with technology because they didn't get on board with it until it was too late.

Innovation from Desperation

Innovation and living your life will always be a balancing act in your life nd trying to find harmony with both is the mission for everyone. When we are in happy and excited and creative places, new ideas always come flooding in and can be distracting from our goals and take away from living our lives. I don't regret for a moment taking the break to be a wife and a new mother, I can't get that time back. But I also knew there was a steep learning curve ahead for me once I decided to dive back in. Sometimes, harmonies can have more powerful notes but with practice and time, they can come together to make sweet music.

How do you find harmony in your ideas and life? I am sure you are thinking "Desiree, what does this have to do with social media?" Well, it is easy to let living your life become about capturing it for the gram. Harmony is taking a selfie with your family and maybe of your delicious food, but then putting your phone away to enjoy the moment and post later.

Share your secrets or hopes for harmony in your life by tagging me @MrsDesireeRose with #shareyourinnovation on social media.

CHAPTER 9

FINDING PURPOSE

I was so amped up. You know that feeling you get when your favorite song comes on while you are in the car. You crank it up, roll down the windows (because it's also always sunny when this happens), and sing and dance like no one is watching.

Or, like when your spouse makes the most amazing meal in the world and you are just happy enjoying it. Then, they decide to put you on cloud nine by handing you dessert, and saying those magic words, "I've got the dishes."

Maybe it's when you get to cuddle and play with a puppy and they are just pure excitement, and happiness. It is just so infectious.

Well, for me it felt like all three of those things were rolled up into one.

I spent a month getting everything mapped out for a brand-spanking new business that was going to solve two problems.

Number one, small business owners are busy running their companies and don't have time to worry about posting on social media. So many of them are busy working IN their business that the idea of working ON their business is secondary. They are experts at what they do, plus they already have a lot of additional challenges. Such as accounting, paperwork, legal compliance with state and federal laws, managing employees, and so on; it's just too much. How are they expected to market their business when they have no freaking idea how to do it? And how are they supposed to afford to outsource this important task when they can't afford NOT to be on social media?

Secondly, military spouses want to work and make money now. They also need a company that understands their life, limitations, lingo, and struggles. They want to be useful beyond baking for a local base fundraiser, taking care of their kids, or managing the never-ending pile of laundry. They want purpose and something for themselves too.

All of these factors led to the birth of All-In-One Social Media.

All-In-One Social Media lets business owners do what they do best — that is, run their business. But I wanted our services to include more than just daily postings to Facebook and Twitter. There were plenty of companies out there that offered posting and just farmed the work out overseas, which often resulted in a lack of understanding of their client's business as well as language barriers. I always thought that was a terrible deal because it wasn't personalized. Plus, in 2015, just posting for its own sake wasn't a valid strategy anymore. You could argue that it did give an online presence by keeping your social media lights on, but it was just so lifeless and without a clearly defined goal.

Then, I saw a post from my friend Gelie, the founder of NetworkPhoenix.com. It's amazing how the right people always show up just when you need them. In my case, Gelie popped up again in my life just as she had six years ago. Every year, she hosts a gigantic networking event that is the talk of the town in Phoenix and a must attend for any entrepreneur. In this case, she was starting to hype her upcoming event by talking about one of her sponsors, Design Pickle.

Innovation from Desperation

Design Pickle was new to the scene in 2015, but were offering an incredible service of unlimited design work for a low flat fee. As a graphic designer since 2001, this blew my mind, but what they were doing was on track with the same thing I was building. That is, a low cost, but effective service, that gives value to business owners so they can focus on their core business.

Like I said, I didn't want to just post on the behalf of clients merely for the sake of posting, I wanted the content to have value and be on brand. Could Design Pickle be the solution I was looking for? Could I use their service to create custom graphics for my customers?

I rabbit holed into this new business possibility, and spent time talking with the Design Pickle sales team. I was candid with them about what I was doing and how I wanted Design Pickle to be a part of it. Their answer was a simple, "Yes." I was over the moon about this pending partnership, and I still credit Design Pickle's existence as one of the big reasons my agency still exists. But I needed just a little more. That frosting on the cake, if you will.

I was now able to allow business to have an online presence WITH branded content, but I wanted to push it over the edge to make sure that branded content was going to be seen, because social media newsfeeds tend to be cluttered.

I look at it his way. If newsfeeds were one of the rooms in my house, they would be my kids' play room. Everything is scattered everywhere. Most of it is forgotten, and without fail there is some trash in there making it an even bigger and smellier mess. But the things that always stand out are the favorites. Those are the toys that get extra love and attention. The question is how is cutting through the clutter on social media accomplished?

Paid Ads!

I researched, took some courses, and spiraled somewhat obsessively on YouTube. I wanted to learn how I could inexpensively run effective ads for my customers. I even tested it out on one of my last standing customers from Pink Media (high five me!) I concluded that I could boost one or two of their custom branded posts and get them more attention, engagement, and Likes to their Facebook page for as little as $25 per month.

So, there I had it. My trifecta of what I was going to offer businesses. Daily postings, custom graphics, and $25 in Facebook advertising. And to put a bow on it and keep me competitive in the social media space, I was only going to charge $125 per month.

Was I crazy? You bet!

Innovation from Desperation

Did I VASTLY undervalue myself? Obviously!

Could you talk me out of it? Nope!

Keep in mind that one of the reasons Stephen and I chose the military life was that I was sick of the grind that came from running my own business. I was tired of pleading with prospects to work with me, then chasing them down to pay their invoices. For six years I had been told over and over, "Oh, I just can't afford that." Hearing that repeatedly messed me up, and if I am honest, it still is something I struggle with. I always get so bummed out when I don't land a client that I am really excited to work with because my services are beyond their budget.

But in 2015, my logic was to get a little bit of money from a lot of people. That way if I lost one, two, or even ten customers, it would not be a devastating blow to my business revenue stream. Plus, if a business didn't have $125 per month to spend on all I was offering, they were NOT a customer I wanted to work with.

Before I could bring military spouses onboard to do the work, I would need to bootstrap this myself. I needed to make sure that I could cover the cost of Design Pickle, and ensure that this would grow my business.

During the month of August, 2015, I spent every weekend parking my pregnant butt at my local Starbucks, hopped up on tea, building this new business.

I created a plan, using GoDaddy's website template builder to map out what All-In-One did, and just put it all together.

On September 1, (the start of my third trimester, I might add) I emailed everyone I knew, telling them that All-In-One Social Media was open for business. We were offering social media marketing for $125 per month, which included daily Facebook and Twitter posts, three to five custom graphics, and a $25 Facebook ad budget.

I got a great response, signing up 15 customers my first month!

All those years of networking, had allowed for me to build an amazing community of not only business owners, but other marketing professionals. Many of them hated doing social media, but their customers asked them to do it for them. I knew this, and made sure that I had a plan in place to work with resellers. This would mean that All-In-One would be the social media team for that agency and we would work under their umbrella. But the customer would never know that another company was doing the work. We wouldn't communicate directly with those customers in any way and just charged the agency the $125 a month, while they marked it up however, they chose to.

I was elated. Based on the success of my first

month, if things kept going this way, I was going to be able to start training and hiring military spouses in December, just three months after launching the new venture.

Then, something happened that stopped me dead in my tracks. My baby stopped moving.

MOMENT OF INNOVATION

There are so many things to unpack in this chapter, not to mention that hardcore cliffhanger! LOL. But it is important to remember that no matter how long you have been doing something or watching someone else do it, that doesn't mean it's right. Like I said in the beginning, you have to innovate to stay ahead. When I was looking around seeing all those scammy businesses succeeding, I realized I couldn't ethically do something like that.

Find a way to be innovative in your industry, so you stand out and grow on your own terms. I am not saying you should reinvent the wheel, but research what you can do to offer great value at a price you are comfortable with, and that will generate the results you want.

I created a mission-driven company that helps businesses get results and save time. Remember, "stop doing shit you hate?" Those who hate doing their own social media are the people I help! What makes me different is not just the service, but WHO is doing the work. Y'all need to grasp something. Social media marketers are a dime a dozen. I go to Social Media Marketing World every year. Of those who attend, eight out of 10 are some type of social media specialist. But not ONE of them put military spouses to work as social media managers. I watch people's entire body language change when I tell them what we do and how we do it. Why? Because so many people can relate to it. They know someone in the service, served themselves, or have a friend, sister, or cousin who is a military spouse.

By being different, I can break down barriers, and go where no one else has been able to, by getting to the next level of the conversation.

What makes you different? What is going to make people go, "OMG! WOW! That's amazing!" Let your mission and purpose be your show stopper. Allow your unique method of getting results to be what keeps them paying that invoice and returning to you.

Share with me your inspiring purpose by tagging me on social media @mrsdesireerose, #shareyourinnovation.

CHAPTER 10
IS MY BABY ALIVE?

Monday, October 5th, started the same way every morning had started for me. My 17-month-old son awoke at 5:00 am, crying for a bottle. I waddled to his room, gave it to him, and, of course, stopped at the bathroom. After all, I was 35 weeks pregnant! However, this time one thing was different. There were no baby kicks. Every morning for 15 weeks, my belly would go crazy by the time I walked back from my son's bed to go pee, but today there was nothing.

My logical mind kicked in, and I went into problem-solving mode. I went downstairs to the fridge and got some orange juice. I chugged and waited. And waited. And waited some more. Nothing.

I went back upstairs to wake up my husband. One of the people in his shop had recently moved to a new base and left us with an at-home heartbeat monitor. I told Stephen to get it. We spent the next five minutes looking for a heartbeat.

Nothing.

We looked at each other, and telepathically had an entire conversation with our eyes. We instinctively knew what to do next. Get dressed, grab my son, some random boxes of food, the diaper bag, and our phone chargers. Get in the car, and drive as fast as possible to the hospital.

I drove. The last thing I needed was for my husband to drive. He was panicked enough as it was, and I needed something to focus on versus worrying about what could be wrong. I pulled up to the front of the hospital and literally leaped out of the car after barely putting it in park. I went to the fourth-floor maternity ward.

"I haven't felt my baby move since last night," I told them.

It was 7:00 a.m.

The staff took me into a room, pulled up my shirt, strapped me in, and found a steady heartbeat. I was so relieved. That is, until they said, "this isn't right." When your baby is in the womb, you do NOT want a steady heartbeat once you hit the third trimester. The heartbeat should be fast, signaling movement and activity.

It was 7:30 a.m.

The ultrasound technicians were called up to my room to see if they could get the baby to move. They tried for 30 minutes. The heartbeat was still steady. It was time to have a baby.

As you know by now, I am a problem solver. I suspected for almost my entire pregnancy that my baby was going to come early. I just had a feeling, so I put a plan into place. My mom was going to arrive the Friday before my scheduled C-Section on November 2. My OBGYN didn't think it was safe to try to give birth naturally with my second child since I had to have an emergency c-section with my son. As part of my emergency plan, I arranged for one of the women in my husband's shop to watch our son in the event I went into labor early.

Again, my husband and I looked at each other, and he took action. Stephen pulled out his phone to call our stand-by babysitter while grabbing the stroller that was holding my son. He hurriedly ran out of the hospital to hand him off to her at our house. It was a 20-minute drive, which meant we were looking at 45 minutes before Stephen could get back. That was about the amount of time my OBGYN needed to get ready for surgery.

It was 8:00 a.m.

While my husband took care of getting our son to the sitter, I was put into prep mode. That meant changing into a hospital gown and pulling my hair back into a braid with a rubber band. While they continued the preparation, I had one thing left to do.

I had to email my clients. Yep, while I was about to have an emergency c-section to deliver my baby five weeks early, I was worried about my clients and business.

I remember very distinctly typing a message while being moved from the hospital room bed to one with wheels that would take me to the operating room.

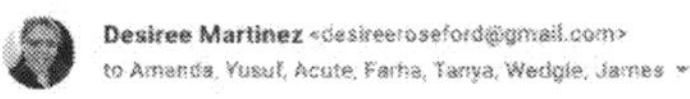

Desiree Martinez <desireeroseford@gmail.com> Mon, Oct 5, 2015, 8:28 AM
to Amanda, Yusuf, Acute, Farha, Tanya, Wedgie, James

Having My baby a month early. Sorry for any delay in communication or lapse in posts.

I'll keep you posted.

--
Desiree Martinez
c: 303.832.3019

Sent from cell phone. Please excuse my bad spelling and crazy autocorrect.

I remember feeling incredibly happy that I had planned and scheduled all the content for the entire month of October that Saturday. But I was also pissed that I didn't have a military spouse or two in the wings ready to do the social media work. How the hell was I going to run my business from the hospital? Would I be emotionally capable? What if my baby died? What would happen to my business then?

Needless to say, it was an intense ride from my room to the operating room. Thank God my husband showed up as they were rolling me into the OR. It was funny to see him putting on his gown while running down the hallway. Up to this point, I had managed to stay in good spirits. I had even joked about how the baby was going to have a cool birthday of 10/5/15. Yes, I was doing math while sitting on the bed, getting ready to be numbed from the waist down, which is standard C-section protocol.

Then, the anesthesiologist told me that I had too much scar tissue from my last epidural, and he was going to have to put me under. I was not surprised because the anesthesiologist from my first childbirth experience was a total idiot who was mean and had no idea how to do his job. That would not be the case this time around. Because I would be put under, my husband wasn't going to be allowed to be in the room. That was when I lost it. I cried and cried and got really scared.

When the doctor came in, they escorted my poor husband to the waiting room, where he was all alone. No family, no friends, not even someone from his shop. Everything had happened so quickly that no one had time to join him at the hospital. I was also alone and still crying. I asked the anesthesiologist if he would hold my hand until I went under. With incredibly kind eyes, he held my hand while I drifted off to sleep.

I did not dream, because I think I was too worried and scared.

When I woke up, I desperately hit the call button on my bed for the nurse. I needed to know what happened to my baby. When the nurse walked in, I only had one question.

"Is my baby alive?" I asked through a dry mouth and with incredible weakness.

"Yes," she said with a smile.

My daughter had wrapped the umbilical cord around her neck twice and was born blue. It took the doctor and NICU team 45 minutes to get her breathing and her color back to normal. My OBGYN later came to the room to sit with me, hold my hand, and tell me through tears of her own, "We tell mother's all the time to come in if they are worried about their babies so we can give them peace of mind. But you saved your baby's life by coming in. I have never seen a baby survive who had the cord wrapped around their neck as much or as tight as your baby."

I began sobbing.

It took what felt like a million years before I was wheeled into the NICU to meet my daughter. My husband had been by her side the moment he was able to, and I could tell that he was hooked. When I saw her, I did that weird smile-crying that only a new mom does. It was really scary seeing her in a plastic bubble with tubes and cables everywhere, but she was alive.

I spent the next two weeks in and out of the NICU. Most of my time was spent doing skin-to-skin bonding, pumping breast milk, then training her how to breastfeed, while advocating for her to those who were trying to hold her back. When I wasn't in NICU, I was sleeping in random places around the hospital and working in the coffee shop.

In between naps for both my daughter and me, her feedings, and diaper changes, I was literally generating and scheduling content for clients. My mom came to visit five-days into our NICU stay to give my husband some relief. He had taken over watching our son, managing the house, taking care of the dogs, and continuously driving back-and-forth between the base and the hospital.

Fourteen days after the scariest moment of my life,

we brought our daughter home, and the real work began. My gratitude to my NICU doctor and nurses can't be expressed in words. I will always be eternally grateful to my doctor for her care and experience to make the delivery a success. My love for my husband deepened as he handled all of the turmoil without complaining. His actions cemented him as a superhero in my eyes forever. And I am also proud of myself for being aware of what was going on with my body. I'm happy that I followed my instincts to get help for my baby and ultimately save her life.

MOMENT OF INNOVATION

Look, there is no amount of planning in the world that can help you when emergencies happen. Trauma, death, fires, premature deaths, a plague of locusts, blood raining down from the sky, your internet going out (seriously, the WORST), emergencies are emergencies. These are the things we do everything in our power to prepare for and prevent, but when they hit, they really rock your cage.

During these times, remember two things. One, let yourself feel what is happening. When my daughter was in the incubator strapped with tubes and things that beeped a lot, I was a wreck. Feeling overwhelming joy that she was alive, and fear that she might die, and longing to just hold her. I know my husband had a world of feelings too and we just had to feel them and live them. That is all you can do to get through those moments.

Two, trust in your people. My mom booked a flight out as soon as she could. My friends from afar ordered me food and my local friends watched my son and did a food train for us. Even my clients sent me kind messages and gave me astronomical amounts of grace while in the hospital. Your people are vital to your mental and emotional success. They want to help take on your pain and your burdens so you can heal.

I don't have much social media or professional advice in this chapter and I am okay with that. Because part of our professional journey is also about the life we are working so hard to live.

How has an emergency derailed your life? I would love it if you trusted me with your story so I can help lift you up. Tag me in your story @mrsdesireerose with #shareyourinnovation on social media (or in this case, maybe the DMs).

CHAPTER 11
DEPLOYMENT AND TRAUMA

Six months after my daughter was born, Stephen got a text message from his shop chief telling him that he would be deployed in the next two months. It is one of those things that all military families eventually face. But every single time it happens, it still comes as a shock. There are so many emotions for everyone involved, on top of all the preparation that has to go into it.

While Stephen prepared to deploy to Africa, I had

to have ACL surgery. An old injury had resurfaced, making it difficult to walk. You know what makes a deployment ten times worse? Being limited physically! Not being able to go up and down the stairs in your own house because of your injury. We were on a crazy schedule of surgery, going to physical therapy, breastfeeding, and changing diapers. There were briefings, packing uniforms, chasing my toddler, signing life insurance policies and last wills and testaments, shopping, and going away parties. It was a blur for both of us.

Deployment

My husband left in early May, one day after our daughter gave him an amazing gift. She said her first words, "Dada," before he left. I cried. A lot. I hugged Stephen goodbye and whispered into his ear, "you'd better come home," gave him one hell of a kiss goodbye, shut the door and slumped down to the floor in tears.

I was a mess and depressed the entire four months he was gone. I kept all the stress and pressure from the birth, recovery, surgery, and deployment bottled up inside of me. I basically lived on the couch when I wasn't serving as a food-source, maid, or toy. I could not wait for bedtime when I just numbed out in front of the TV. I remember begging and pleading with my friend who ran the Mother's Day Out program at a local church to let me have a spot for my kids so I could get a break. (For those of you that don't know, Mother's Day Out is an amazing program in Texas churches that give mothers time to be alone about several hours, twice a week). Most mothers with young kids don't work and have several small kids, so the program is widespread and a total lifesaver.

I finally got into the program, and it literally saved my life and my business. Every Tuesday and Thursday from 8:30 a.m. until 2:30 p.m., I was kid-free. I would drive down the street, grab two breakfast burritos (the kind that you can only get from a small hut in a parking lot), and went to Starbucks. I worked with more focus and gusto than I ever had in my entire life.

I tackled emails, conducted sales calls, participated in social media conversations, and was a glimmer of the person I wanted to be. That is, a professional woman making a difference in the world. I wasn't about to fall victim to unpreparedness like I had when I was surprised by the sudden birth of my daughter. To avoid that scenario, I hired two military spouses to handle the workload. I spent months systemizing the onboarding process for new clients and handing them off to my team.

Once someone signed up for our service, they received an email along with a questionnaire for us to learn about their business. We needed to know who they were, what they were about, and more, so we could represent them on social media accurately. We would also gather logos and existing marketing materials for design inspiration. We walked them through how to make me an administrator of their Facebook page and how to give us their Twitter login info. Once we had what we needed, we would start posting content for them, usually within 48 hours. At this point, I would forward all the information to the account manager. We would also add their accounts to our social media management software. We utilized Sendible, the best and only tool I will use for this task. Then, the girls would get started.

I had spent much time doing the actual work at the start of All-In-One. Plus, I had five years of social media experience under my belt. Still, I needed to clone myself (well, my knowledge) for my team members. I started conducting one-on-one training via Zoom, but ultimately created a series of videos showing how it all worked. Think of it as a 101 course on how to be a social media manager, but only for my team. After all, I had to keep my "secret sauce" in-house!

Having a system for training my team and onboarding clients was a lifesaver. I cannot emphasize this enough because if I didn't have this in place, my agency and all the hopes and dreams that I had attached to it would have gone belly up.

Like I said, I was a mess.

Desiree Martinez

My depression peaked in August. I had just spent four-weeks in Phoenix "visiting" my friends and family. I put visiting in quotations because it wound up being a waste of my time and money. What they don't tell you about going home is that life goes on without you. I spent my days waiting around for people to be available to hang out with me. But they were working, taking care of their families, and managing their lives. They all tried to find time to spend with me, but all my expectations were blown up. It was100 percent my fault. I was just so desperate for people, help, and relief that it made everything just horrible.

My two-year-old was going through sleep regression and was awake much of the night. He would also wake up screaming. At the same time, my daughter started teething. and the only thing that fixed her was breastfeeding. So, between being lonely and spending all my time waiting, I also wasn't sleeping.

Within eight hours of returning to Texas, I woke up in the middle of the night, unable to breathe. I couldn't lay down at all and ended up sleeping almost vertical until I could go to the base clinic to get checked out. My neighbor was kind enough to watch my son, and I took my daughter to my appointment. They ended up hooking me up to an EKG machine to monitor my heartbeat.

It was irregular.

Innovation from Desperation

I was told I needed to go to the hospital, and I couldn't take my daughter with me.

Who the hell was I supposed to call to take care of her? I didn't have a network of people that I could turn to and trust to watch my nursing baby. I had spent the last 18 months being pregnant, a food-source, or both. Oh, and I started a company. Who the hell has time for people?

I ended up calling my husband's shop and asking for help. One of his co-workers had a daughter a little older than mine. She was able to get her while I was taken to the hospital in an ambulance.

At the hospital, they ran all kinds of tests, while I just waited around for the results. Oh, and I was getting calls and messages from people saying they couldn't watch my son anymore because they had to go to work. So, they had to pass him off to someone else.

Meanwhile, I had to have a procedure done where they put dark liquid into my veins to look at my arteries and my heart. Of course, that left me unable to breastfeed for 24-hours. Thank god for my fridge full of breastmilk! I also learned that I had to stay overnight at the hospital for monitoring.

I had to call the couple watching my daughter asking if they could watch her overnight. I had to walk them through where to get more breast milk, diapers (we cloth-diapered both my kids), and clothes. They had to rummage through my house to get what they needed. My son ended up staying with a friend of mine who was going through a divorce but still had base access. She stayed at my house with my son and dog. She had to go to work in the morning and would pass my son off to one of the guys in my husband's shop.

Yes, it was a lot to handle! I share it with you so you can truly understand the scope of worry and stress my mind was under while my husband was on the other side of the world. Imagine his shock and worry when he got word from his commander that his wife was in the hospital.

Let that all sink in for a minute.

By morning I was raging. You might think, "well, at least you got some sleep." Nope! The hospital staff woke me up every few hours to check my vitals. In the morning, I told my nurse that she needed to get a doctor into my room in the next 15 minutes. Otherwise, I was walking out of the hospital because strangers were watching my babies.

"My husband is fighting for our country on the other side of the world while you dick around with paperwork," I told her. "And NO, I don't have family in town, we are a goddamn military family!"

Five minutes later, I had a doctor, a diagnosis, my prescription was being filled, and discharge papers were being processed.

This trauma and depression would be something I would have to work on for over a year with a therapist and medication. If I had not had a system in place for my business, my hopes and dreams of helping military spouses, while providing for small businesses, would have gone up in smoke.

Find Your Tribe

I am a people person. My energy comes from the energy of others. If I could start every day with a great conversation, I would truly be unstoppable. In the midst of all the craziness of being a mother of two, I found the Mothers of Preschoolers (MOPS) program.

Traditionally, MOPS operates through a church, and I am an agnostic. I believe in a higher power, just not a specific one. So, I always felt weird going to a program at a church. But I needed people. I needed adult conversation and delicious food that I didn't make. I also needed direction in the crazy thing we call motherhood, paired with zero judgment. MOPS became that for me.

After my summer of hell, I returned to MOPS, beat down but relieved to have several kid-free hours to be around moms who were also struggling, beat up, and looking for support. I got matched up with four amazingly different women who "got me." I could make nerdy Star Trek references, and they actually understood them. It turns out that they all had come off of really terrible summers. They were so relieved to find our group, where they could connect with others and openly vent.

They were totally normal while extraordinary at the same time. College- educated, but mothers with ambitions and a sense of lostness marinated in sassiness and humor. They were my people. In my time of pure and utter lowness, these women helped build me up with text messages, swapping war stories, nights out, and just a sense of togetherness. We really couldn't have been more different, but we bonded through our need for support and love that had nothing to do with kids or husbands.

I share this with you to remind you that you need people apart from those at work or your business. Having people like this will keep you grounded and away from the trap of immersing yourself in your work bubble. They will keep you interesting and informed about the outside world. They can give you the love, support, and perspective you need to move forward with your goals and ambitions.

Find your tribe and hold them close. Make time for them. Be vulnerable and raw with them. No matter what life throws at you, these are the people that will be there for you at every one of your celebrations and failures. Everyone needs this.

Now put this book down and dust off that text chat you have with your tribe and send them a message or joke that only they would understand. To my tribe, Avengers Assemble!

Trauma

Stephen's deployment really messed me up but wound up doing more damage to him. His homecoming was as happy a time as you can imagine, but there were some telling signs that there was some serious healing that needed to happen. For example, he didn't want the kids to be there when I picked him up from the airfield. He didn't want there to be any chance of them remembering that daddy was away. He couldn't sleep. His temper was short. He just couldn't stop worrying about being called to deploy again.

One day in early November, he came home in tears. His name was posted for a scheduled June deployment. He was having an actual panic attack telling me about it. He continued telling me that he talked to his shop chief and supervisor about how he was feeling. They just looked at him and said, "This is the job! Look, it's just a six-month deployment. What would happen if you got sent to South Korea? That's a year. You'll be okay."

I knew he couldn't do another deployment, but something in that statement stuck out to me. South Korea. What would happen if he got orders to South Korea? Then a smile crept across my face.

I got down on our kitchen floor, looked at him with my smile and said, "but what if you did get sent to South Korea? We could go with you!" He was super confused.

Here's what you need to know about being a military family. The government owns the service member, NOT the family. We are very graciously called "dependents" (can we all slow eye roll together)? Most of the time, we can't go with our service member to combat areas like Afghanistan, Africa or Turkey. But we could go to a place like South Korea. It was a first world country with plenty of American citizens living a normal life there.

I went into research mode. Would it be possible for my husband to volunteer to go to Korea, so that we could live near him off base? It seemed like such a shot in the dark. But I am a problem solver who almost always gets her way. There had to be a way.

It turns out this happens all the time. In fact, surprise, surprise, there was a Facebook group of military spouses living in South Korea. They were non-command sponsored, meaning the active duty spouse is stationed there, you live there, but had to pay your own way. We could get paid a housing allowance to live off base based on rank and COLA, which is extra money to cover the additional costs of living overseas. The military would pay for Stephen's trip, while we just had to pay our own way to South Korea on a commercial flight.

This was the answer! My husband could volunteer to "deploy" to South Korea, and we would live off base as so many other families did. This was a widespread practice to get what is called "Base of Preference," where before leaving for South Korea, you have follow-on orders to a base of your choice. Most people pick a cool overseas base like Yakota, Japan, or Aviona, Italy.

This option would prevent Stephen from being put through the trauma of being deployed again, away from his family.

On November 21, 2016, Stephen came home and told me he had orders to deploy to South Korea with a report date of no later than June 1, 2017. We would be joining him there.

We did it. We found a way to stay together as a family, but now I just needed to figure out how in the hell was I going to grow my business from the other side of the world.

MOMENT OF INSPIRATION

Systems, system, SYSTEMS!

Like you saw in the last chapter, I was totally thrown for a massive curveball when my daughter was born prematurely. I knew that I needed to ensure I had systemized as many things possible because my life would always have inconsistencies because of motherhood and military life.

It is important for you to do something crucial for you, your brand, or your business...Are you listening?

Don't let everything revolve around you!

This applies to so many things: your income, work, taxes, legal protection, even your content marketing strategy. If everything you do is like a light switch where you are either on and everything is working or you are off and nothing is, what are you supposed to do when your light bulb burns out?

What you really need to do is be more like a car where you might need to initially turn it on to get it running, once it is going all the parts of the car work together to accomplish the end goal, to move the car. You can steer, speed up, slow down, or even park the car, but it will still keep running.

If you are the end and beginning of your success you will fail! Harsh, but true. You never know what life or circumstance is going to throw at you, so you need to make sure you can protect income. If your income isn't protected the rest of your existence isn't either. What happens if you lose your job? What happens if someone dies? What happens if a pandemic happens and you lose over half of your business? What happens if something happens to you? "What happens if?" needs to be at the forefront of your mind when making your money moves.

What happened when I lost my job at CBS 5? We ended up going into the military which gave us some financial freedom to figure out what to do next, but came with a new world of struggles. We made the decision from a place of zero preparedness. You don't want to be in this sort of position, trust me.

The same can be said for your content marketing. While you are responsible for establishing the voice and tone of your online marketing, if you have the right system and team in place you will be able to continue to be "the voice" of the brand, while someone else can execute your vision.

And before you @ me with your "but Desiree that requires money" talk, I want you to remember that once you become financially invested in your development (personal or professional) you are likely to take it seriously and succeed. It's called putting skin in the game for a reason.

Creating systems will allow for you to make the moves you want to make and live the life you want, while also protecting you when life happens. Because it isn't a matter of if, it is a matter of when.

What systems do you want to add to your life so you can work on high-level projects to move forward? Share them with me @mrsdesireerose with #shareyourinnovation on social media so I can help hold you accountable to accomplish those big moves.

CHAPTER 12
IT WAS HORRIBLE, BUT I DID IT!

What I love about my job is how many amazing and different people I get to "meet" online. I am probably connected to hundreds of people that have influenced me, or that I have influenced. Most of them I have never had a voice-to-voice conversation with, let alone met in person. The same is true for many of my clients. I have never met or had a conversation with them either.

Around the time we were learning that we were going to move to the other side of the world, one guy named Vincenzo kept showing up in my social media newsfeed. He was promoting the live streams he was doing and also Amy Schmittauer's upcoming book, "Vlog Like A Boss." I Friended Vincenzo and started watching the videos that Amy was putting up on YouTube.

Now, I was just not that into YouTube. I had absolutely nothing against it; I just hadn't gravitated toward it. I liked Facebook and started getting on Instagram more, especially after they rolled out their Stories feature. My husband, however, LOVED YouTube. He was always trying to show me some funny video, or learn how to do or fix something, courtesy of a YouTube "how-to" video.

But Amy was slowly giving me an education about YouTube without me even knowing it. She was teaching me about vlogging, which was blogging with video. She was teaching me things I needed to know, one video at a time. Every Tuesday, Thursday, and Sunday, I was learning from her. She even had a name for me. I was one of her "socials." Even better, she had a book coming out, entitled, "Vlog Like A Boss," which I bought. But not before watching every single video she put up during the month of January as a part of her book launch.

Y'all, that book was a game-changer for me. I read Amy's book in between packing up our lives. I was also running my agency, training new team members, breastfeeding, potty training (hallelujah), and watching Moana for the bazillionth time. Every page was solid gold. I could feel myself getting smarter as I read every page.

I finished the book, filling it with highlights, notes, and stickers. Then, I turned to Stephen and said, "I'm going to start a YouTube channel!" Ever supportive, he replied, "Great idea! But maybe wait until we get to South Korea. You don't need another thing on your plate." And he was right. But I obsessed over my new YouTube channel for the next four months. FOUR months!

I had a plan!

YouTube was going to be how I grew my agency while living on the other side of the world. I would create videos teaching people how to function on social media. Anything from how to find or do things on the different platforms, to tools I loved. I would even share how I created content and made the magic for my clients. I was going to give the milk away.

Why? Because I have NEVER made money as a social media marketer by showing people how to do it. I have (and still) make money by doing it for them! The purpose of my channel would be to help fledgling businesses stand out in a cluttered news feed by solving their social media problems. But the goal would be to overwhelm them with how much it is to do social media. Hopefully, they would then hire my agency to do it for them.

At the end of April 2017, we finally left Dyess. The process was like pulling teeth, and often felt like it was never going to happen. Stephen's command staff pulled him aside and told him how dangerous it would be to take his family to Korea. They told him he was a terrible father and husband for taking us to Korea because they thought it was "an undeveloped country and war zone." But after signing a waiver from his command advising against taking us to South Korea, they handed him his orders and we peaced out. I thought the warning against moving to South Korea was ridiculous, as Korea is a first world country with more technological advancements than America. The country has one of the world's best education systems, boasts the 11th largest economy in the world, and the fourth largest cinema industry. They were clearly either uninformed or uneducated.

For the next month, we took an amazing cross-country trip to visit family, and just experience and enjoy the wonders of America. We flew out of Los Angeles International on May 30 for our new adventure in South Korea. Our entourage included two adults, two toddlers, one emotional support dog, a lot of luggage and carry-on baggage.

There is something you need to know about me. I

am at home in the world. The crazier the cultural situation is, the more I thrive. I adapt well, dodging and weaving through it all. It took us about a month to get situated in a house, get financially settled and into a routine. I was next- level blessed to move next door to an English-speaking Korean with two kids close to mine in age. Every day, this adorable yellow van would show up and pick her two-year-old son up and then bring him back in the later afternoon. I was fascinated.

In South Korea, they have a population issue. As an incentive to have children, the Korean government offers paid maternity leave and paid childcare until children are old enough to go to school, starting at the age of one. These little yellow buses are all over, taking one- to five-year-old kids to daycare so their mothers can continue working. Which, by the way, is something Korean women fought hard to have the right to do.

She was able to get me into her son's school, which was both totally weird and awesome. They only spoke Korean, so all my communications were through text messages or translated by my neighbor. But every day at 8:00 a.m., the little yellow van came and picked up my kids and brought them home at 4:00 p.m. My children were loved in a way every parent hopes childcare workers will love their children. As a bonus, my children learned Korean, and mommy got to work.

For the first time in my agency's existence, I was able to work on my business a full day every day of the week. It was heavenly! The silence of an empty house was golden, and I could finally start my YouTube channel!

One of the things that made moving to South Korea difficult was we were limited on what we could bring. We were allowed to ship 700 pounds plus whatever we could bring on the plane. That was it. So, the idea of buying and shipping a fancy camera, ring light, and all the extras that the other prominent YouTubers were using wasn't an option for me.

It ended up being a blessing. All I had for my first year on YouTube was a Logitech 1080p webcam, a window, and white walls. I had a room in the upstairs of my house that I turned into an office. I thought I would get crafty and make a cool background by hanging simple things on the walls, but the walls were cement and covered in wallpaper. I tried using command hooks, but the heat just melted the sticky parts off, and the wall hangings fell to the floor. If you go to my YouTube channel (www.YouTube.com/mrsdesireerose) and watch my early videos, you can see my original set and how it just becomes less and less.

I was going to launch my YouTube channel the bootstrap way, with what I had (which is what I still tell people to do). Now, I wasn't only going to start doing YouTube, I was going to make it a whole thing.

I launched my YouTube channel with VEDA – Vlog Every Day in August. I did so because Amy did it, and it seemed like an excellent way to start. On August 1, 2017, I posted my first YouTube video, and launched my podcast, Marketing for Your Business. I recorded 31 videos throughout the month of August and published 10 podcast episodes, recording the videos during the interview and putting them on the channel.

Y'all, my first video was terrible. I was wearing way too much eye makeup. I thought I would be really casual and paired the makeup with a tank top that showed my bra. Not in a cute way, but in a sloppy way (*facepalm*). I was also sweaty, and you can see me getting wetter by the minute. Why, you ask? Because, while I had a dedicated office, it also had no air conditioning. That's because Koreans have air conditioners in the common rooms, but don't have central air. So, in July, it was in the high 90s to low 100s with 90 to 100 percent humidity, and my plus-size butt was sweatin'. My webcam was also mounted to my laptop as most people do, and I had to sit to film. Because I am a hand talker, there is lots of hitting the desk and camera shaking.

I'm a mess, my info was right, but I did it. I hit record and kept recording. I went on to have weeks and weeks of bad videos. And then months of bad videos. And even when I found a rhythm, bought a small cheap tripod for my webcam, and moved to film by the window, I still made bad videos.

But with each filming session, I got a little better. I would apply a new technique, make a small change, or improve one small thing. I got better at framing, sound, and my speaking pattern. I fumbled less, dressed better, and sweated less. Gradually my videos improved, one video at a time.

I showed up online three times a week. I was giving tutorials, sharing my podcast recordings, and walking viewers through how to do things. I also experimented with different ideas to see if they would work. I did a monthly Military Marketing video where I would share information about military life. My hope was marketers would learn more about military life, and come up with ways to better market to us (Truth be told, I was really just sick of seeing bad military advertising). Those random videos were killing me with the algorithm, so I started doing them every Monday. Even then, it was a failed experiment. My hope of being a military marketing expert wasn't working and confused YouTube's analytics. They couldn't figure out how to showcase me.

I also started to do different types of series videos. My first one shared monthly content marketing ideas. I would give ideas each month of what people could post, such as holidays, traditions, did you knows, and that sort of thing. It took a whole year to do, and I also included fun stuff like Christmas, Halloween, and Star Wars Day. These were popular series, and I still get hits on those videos depending on the time of year.

At the beginning of 2018, I did a Social Media for Beginners series, where I broke down what each online platform looked like and how it should be used. The goal for this nine-part series was view and binge-watching, along with feeding my opt-in through my Social Media Setup Checklist. By the end of the year, I had thousands of views across all the videos, and my email list added hundreds of members to it. This was my first time thinking through a full strategy for YouTube that had longevity and an off-platform Call to Action. It allowed me to collect emails, with the hope of eventually selling to those new members.

With every video, I got more views and added more subscribers to my email list. I also started getting asked to be on other people's podcasts and live shows. And then that magic moment happened.

I started getting requests for my services.

Alan Spicer
YouTube Broke My Heart

Alan Spicer is a UK based YouTube Certified Expert and educator, tea drinker, cat lover, wrestling junkie, and stats junkie. Since 2017, Alan has educated others on how they can "start creating" on YouTube. With hundreds of videos and millions of hours of watch time, Alan has positioned himself as a leading UK YouTube educator that has given him professional growth and financial freedom.

YouTube truly is a rollercoaster, and I have experienced their wild highs and their gut-clenching lows as they drop out from under you. I have always had an eye on the future when it comes to social media. Even when I was a bright-eyed, bushy-tailed, baby faced 19-year-old lad, I was still dabbling with growing a Pro Wrestling fan forum.

This love of social media never left me. It guided me into web development, search engine optimization, and in the long run, a curiosity into this "web video thing."

To start with, YouTube was a tool that I wanted to learn to see how it could help my clients. The idea was that if I could learn how to make videos and to get them to rank on Google, maybe I could sell this service as a plugin to my web development and SEO packages.

The problem was this… I got addicted to the making videos part!

In 2013, I started my first YouTube channel. Like most new YouTubers, I had no idea what the channel was about and absolutely no idea how to promote it. I put out my first cringe-worthy video introducing myself on a shaky compact camera from my crappy little apartment. The lighting was orange, the audio was terrible, and you could see the mound of dirty plates in the background.

Nobody ever tells you how addictive something can be until you fall in love with a hobby.

For weeks and months, I toiled away, uploading lifestyle commentaries, rants, and movie reviews. The initial plan of just learning how to upload and try to master the SEO for the web development business had faded into the back of my mind. I was hooked, and I just wanted to make videos.

Over the next five years, I stumbled across the niche that would work for me, funny news. Every morning I would wake up, flick through the online papers, and weird news forums. These became the fuel and the topics of my content.

The MrHairyBrit channel grew to 40,000+ subscribers and over 40 million views. I learned how to film better videos, share them on social media, and pick great topics to inject with my sense of humor. The problem was that although I had made over 1,200 videos in those five years, it was all in the grey area of the YouTube entertainment niche. So, when YouTube finally started squeezing people out of the grey and into the black and white. I didn't fit anymore, and the channel had to die.

I was CRUSHED, devastated! It was like being dumped out of the blue by the love of your life – heartbroken - five years of hard work, grind, and sacrifice.

My only saving grace was that in the final three to four months of the failing romance with my first channel, I had decided to take my knowledge and start teaching!

I will forever be in love with my first "YouTube soulmate" for many reasons, but the biggest reason is the lessons I learned in growing that channel. I was able to parlay that into my new, more laser-focused dive into the social platform.

This new, fresh outlook on the YouTube platform took me into the YouTube Educator niche. In a strangely curious return to what my initial goals were for YouTube, I would now teach people what I had learned and build a business out of it.

I knew it would be a hard climb to grow in a new niche, but I am stubborn, and now I had some experience in growing a channel. Educational content can be painfully slow to get into, but I was determined to make it work.

Spin forward to the Summer of 2020. I am a YouTube Certified Expert with millions of video views, nearly a thousand subscribers, growing at over 10 percent monthly. The change in niche also came with a bonus that I was more commercially viable for adverts, sponsors, and overall business.

The channel has been live for nearly three years and thanks to the lessons from my last roller coaster ride. I was able to build income streams and business relationships that enabled me to go full time on YouTuber with just 3,000 subscribers.

MOMENT OF INNOVATION

YouTube is a marathon, not a sprint. If you run the race with a plan you can build reputation, establish your authority and even become a very profitable venture, if you put your mind to it. But I wouldn't be where I am today if I hadn't learned how to take the highs with the lows of the YouTube rollercoaster ride.

MOMENT OF INNOVATION

It took a lot of time, dedication, and angry creating. To this day, my YouTube channel is "small" compared to big guys like Social Media Examiner or Amy Schmittauer-Landino. Nevertheless, it is a mighty channel with a wonderful community that trusts me. I am their go-to girl for social media problem solving and content marketing solutions.

My only regret after all these years as a social media marketing is not getting on YouTube sooner. But that doesn't mean that it is too late for you to get started there. YouTube doesn't have anyone like you on their platform because there is only one you. No one does what you do in the way you do it. Share your genius with the world, because we all want to hear from you.

Don't worry about all the other stuff. You're not fat, too weird, or too (insert negative thing here). You are IMPOSSIBLY AMAZING just the way you are. Use what you've got and just hit that record button. You will improve with each video. The longer you are on there, the more you'll want to grow, learn how to do better, figure out the algorithm, obsess about your analytics, and dive into becoming a YouTuber. But NONE of that can happen until you hit record, share your wisdom, and put it out there.

Maybe you are already on YouTube. Ask yourself, what can I do to grow even more? Do I have a promotion strategy beyond being in a constant loop of creating content and working to make the algorithm work best for me? Could I be creating less but doing more with what I have? These are all things to ask yourself when it comes to YouTube.

Because here's the thing. You don't have to be a YouTuber to be successful with video. While I think that every business, brand, or person trying to do something in the world needs to be on YouTube, you do NOT need to be making two or three videos per week. You can speak your truth with just one video a month.

That's right! I said it! Don't @ me, all you YouTube educators!

One video per month can be the foundation of all your content marketing. You just need to use it right. I always say use it once and put it in all the places, so that you can work smart, not hard.

I want to help you with this! Head over to **www.mrsdesireerose.com/30-day**s, where I will hold your hand for 30-days, showing you what to make, where to put it, and how to get leads, all from one video per month.

Where are you with your YouTube journey? Tell me @MrsDesireeRose with #shareyourinnovation on social media.

CHAPTER 13
MILITARY SPOUSE TO BREADWINNER

By the time we left South Korea in June of 2018, I was still madly in love with doing YouTube. I found it easy and natural to create videos to help people. We were headed to our next duty station in Las Vegas, and I was excited to have a dedicated place where I could build a set and buy all the gear to level up my channel.

As I mentioned in the previous chapter, our move to South Korea was primarily to prevent my husband from deploying and being away from us because it had caused him such trauma. But everyday things started to get harder and harder for him. Getting up in the morning to go to work, doing his job, playing with the kids, enjoying things he loves like TV time together and video games. He was becoming short- tempered and just frustrated all the time.

The stress slowly started eating away at him and our marriage. We fought all the time, arguing about how he wasn't happy, and how work made him feel small and insignificant. Still, he operated from a place for fear, afraid of being taken away or kept from us. He couldn't leave work at the door when he came home. Instead, he went through the motions. But you could see he was fighting with his mind to enjoy and love the things that mattered to him.

As his wife, his person that is always there, his ride-or-die, there was nothing I could do to fix him. This destroyed me. I am a fixer, the person that makes him happy, and knows what to do when he is sad to pull him out of it. I am the planner of fun, the executor of silliness, but all I could do through this was yell and be resentful.

We would fight about how things were, and why he couldn't just let it go and focus on the family. The arguments became about how mad he was that I couldn't help him, and how disappointed I was in him, or that he couldn't even get up for his kids. We were angry, and one day it boiled over.

We were again fighting in the bedroom while trying to keep our small kids occupied with a show in the other room. Both Stephen and I were cracking and breaking mentally. I told him, "I can't do this anymore! You need to get help. I can't fix you! I can't be what makes you happy!"

I watched his ears get bright red, and his eyes fill with rage and genuine hatred.

I couldn't do it anymore. I couldn't be the reason someone was happy, because it was just eating away at who I was as a person, a wife, a mother, and a business owner.

We didn't talk for a while, and I honestly don't remember the details of what happened after that. I know that I went into robot-mode and continued to take care of the kids, the house, my business, and the military spouse community obligations I had taken on.

My husband tried to get help. He talked with his flight chaplain and a few different mental health professionals that were available on the base. But he never truly opened up because that fear of being taken away from us still lived in him. He carried this with him to Las Vegas and continued to get counseling. Unfortunately, he still was not able to receive the breakthrough he needed to start healing.

It was during this time that I dabbled in counseling but also dove into self-help books. I read books like "You Are A Badass," by Jen Sincero, "Perfect Is Boring," by Tyra Banks, and "Girl Wash Your Face," by

Rachel Hollis. Other helpful volumes included "We're Going to Need More Wine," by Gabrielle Union, and "What Are the Odds?" By Tisha Marie Pelletier. These books gave me perspective about who I was, what I needed to do, and all the f's I didn't need to give. But the one thing they all preached was that I have to unapologetically take care of myself to be any good to those I love and those that need me.

Throughout this time, I was trying so hard to grow my business, and cool and amazing opportunities would be presented to me. However, I fell short on making them work because the rest of my life was getting in the way. I felt like a crappy mom because all that fighting (even if it was in the other room) was taking me away from my kids. They are only little for such a short time, and while the days were long and exhausting, I knew someday I will look back and regret not being with them more.

I also learned that I couldn't fix other people. That was the hardest lesson and is still something I have to check myself (so I don't wreck myself #hadtosayit). I can't fix my husband's mental health. It is his burden to bear, but for damn sure I am going to be there by his side every step of the way. While I may not be able to fix him, I can be supportive. I can be there when he needs me and fight every urge I have to try and fix or help and just be an ear to listen and arms to hug.

Upon moving back to the States, we were also faced

with a big "now what?" It was going to be our last duty station and final year in the Air Force. Our plan to do the full 20 years and retire went out the window shortly after my husband returned from his first deployment, but we hadn't talked about what to do next.

So back to the ole, "What now?" list we went, but this time we had two kids in tow.

We were sold on the idea of getting an RV and just traveling around the country as a family. This is something I have wanted to do for years. We would figure out where we would want to call our forever home while I continued working remotely., Then one day, Stephen came to me and said, "I want to move to Phoenix. I need help, and I know I can get it there. We have family and friends there, and it is just something I need."

I immediately said okay, and before I could start researching places to live, school zones, and the cost of living, he said one more thing.

"I don't want to work. I want to be a stay-at-home dad."

He explained that he just wasn't mentally healthy enough to handle job pressures, and he didn't want to waste his GI Bill going to school. The six years he was in the Air Force destroyed his confidence, problem-solving skills, memory, and so much more.

I would need to be the sole breadwinner, and had one year to figure out how to do that.

So, while my husband worked his last year in the Air Force, we put our kids into an all-day preschool at our local YMCA. I put my head down and focused on one singular goal: replacing my husband's income.

My road map to accomplishing this included:

Speaking at more events and positioning myself as an expert, sharing my agency's mission and converting the audience members into leads.

Doubling down on YouTube by fine-tuning my message to draw the right people into my community.

Finding more partnerships so I could align myself with brands I love and believe in, and partnering together so I could get paid to work with them and promote them through affiliate marketing.

Speaking

Like I said before, amazing opportunities were starting to present themselves. While I was in Korea, my YouTube channel and podcast allowed me to build credibility amongst my peers. I went to Social Media Marketing World for the first time in 2018. I had wanted to attend since I began seeing my colleagues posting about it in 2014. But, at that time, I was either pregnant or breastfeeding. After the 2017 event, I bought a ticket and told my husband that even though we were going to be in Korea, I was going to attend the 2018 event.

When March of 2018 rolled around, I embarked on a 24-hour journey from our base in South Korea to San Diego, where I had the time of my life! I got to meet online friends IRL, do video segments with people, and learn amazing new things. I even got to meet the one and only Amy Landino, and see her speak for the first of many times.

I was hooked on in-person events and made it a goal to go to more once we returned to the States that June. But I also wanted to challenge myself to land more speaking gigs, so that I could share my truth and experience about social media marketing with others. I made a big ole' list of free conferences locally and nationally that were looking for speakers. I wrote a list of a few different topics and takeaways that I could give tremendous value about and leave the audience wanting more.

I slowly starting booking speaking gigs around the country and spent a lot of 2019 on the road speaking or attending conferences.

YouTube, Part Two

My decision to double down on YouTube was definitely a frustrating journey. When I decided to dive into YouTube, I knew that the only way I would be able to do it was to have an editor. I knew I needed to remove any excuses I might have, such as not having time to edit my videos. I began with a college kid I found on Fiverr. Then, after a wonderful interview for my Marketing for Your Boring Business podcast, Alan took over as my editor and YouTube manager. Now you met Alan in the YouTube chapter, and he still does an amazing job on my videos. But I chose to become obsessed with the backend of my YouTube channel and improve my content. I was still not hitting the mark I wanted.

Because I wasn't specific enough, it took me 18-months to monetize my channel (which requires 1,000 subs and 4,000 hours of watch time). My growth was way slower than I desired, and I needed to level up my strategy. What is so amazing about the YouTube community is that so many people are willing to help you because they want to see you grow. I put my challenges out into the YouTube world and got back so much amazing feedback. Many people gave me actionable steps that allowed me to improve and level up my channel.

I ended up really niching into content marketing,

streamlining my purpose statement (helping your business grow with better content marketing), and focusing on keyword-driven titles. I simplified my thumbnails to have less text and evoke emotion, as well as having quality descriptions.

In the summer of 2019, I went from being a person that used YouTube as a marketing tool to a YouTuber. My channel began the summer with 1,678 subscribers and 145,680 views. By making these thoughtful and intentional changes, my channel jumped to 3,950 subscribers and 350,569 video views by the end of the year! With that growth came a vast increase in my email list, and more people signing up for the All-In-One service. I also saw a rise in customer service requests.

Braille Skateboarding

I attended Video Marketing World in September of 2019. It is a smaller, more intimate video marketing conference that helps small businesses with advice and strategies from gigantic names in the YouTube and video space. One of the sessions was a one-on-one interview with Devin Weber, the CEO of Braille Skateboarding. She is a powerhouse woman who guides a team of skater dudes, helping break down the stereotypes about skateboarders, while also sticking to their mission statement that anyone can skateboard.

I was sitting in the front row, taking in her goodness when she said something that made my ears perk up and my brain start spinning. "We don't know what to do on Facebook. So, if any of you have any ideas, I am all ears!"

I was able to connect with her in the hotel lobby, and in a super not-creepy way, asked if she could come to my hotel room (totally not creepy) to interview for a new podcast I was launching, called "The Women of YouTube." She totally agreed, and we had a killer interview. Right after I stopped recording, I told her, "I have an idea for how you can get on Facebook!" She pulled out her phone to take notes and said, "hit me!"

I suggested that she start a Facebook Group called "Parents of Skateboarders." My idea was to bring together two groups. parents who were skateboarders and now had kids, and parents of skateboarders who were totally freaked out and needed help navigating the world of skateboarding. She loved the idea and said, "So, you're going to handle that for us, right?"

Handled it, I did. I not only launched their community but also stepped in to help breathe life into their Facebook Page. They had more than 130,000 followers but were posting in a half-ass way to that community. Their engagement and views were in the toilet, which made ZERO sense since they have the largest skateboarding channel on YouTube. As I write this book, they had almost five-million subscribers, with that number growing steadily every day.

I threw myself into testing and studying the Facebook analytics, and came up with a posting plan. My plan boosted engagement and followers and allowed them to make money through Facebook's Video Monetization service. As a result, Braille's Facebook Page went from no income to making more than $10,000 a month by April 2020, all from organic traffic, not paid ads.

You have to be on the lookout for great opportunities to fill a void in someone's brand or business. You also can't be afraid to speak up! If you have an idea to help someone, share it, even if there is nothing in it for you. Working with Braille Skateboarding ended up helping my family financially as my husband transitioned out of Air Force life. That wouldn't have happened without me speaking up and giving value to someone else.

Brand Partnerships

This idea took a totally different strategy. I knew how to work an algorithm or get on a stage to convince businesses to work me. But this idea was going to require more one-on-one contact, staying in front of the prospects, and showing them how I could add value to their brand.

There were three brands I really wanted to work with because I loved them so much: Tubebuddy, Sendible and Streamyard.

Tubebuddy

Tubebuddy is a YouTube channel extension that helps ensure your video performs better on the platform. The extension improves the video on the back end, adding things like better keywords, titles, descriptions, thumbnails, and more. I had approached them in February of 2019 with an idea. I was excited about Social Media Examiner making a big deal about going all-in on YouTube. When they announced the speaker lineup for Social Media Marketing World 2019, I was disappointed that all the speakers were men.

While the announced speakers were all powerhouses in the YouTube space, I felt underrepresented. More than 55 percent of marketers are women, so shouldn't a marketing conference at least have one woman speaking on the topic? I actually went to the person who handled all the speaker events and proposed doing a Women of YouTube panel, focusing on why marketers and brands should work with women YouTubers. He loved the idea, but all the sessions had already been booked for the upcoming event. However, he suggested that I do it as a livestream before the event.

As you already know, I'm not one to turn down an opportunity. There was only one brand I could think of that I wanted to work with, and that was Tubebuddy. That previous November, Tubebuddy had done a Women Creator series. I thought my event would be a good tie in with theirs. Within an hour of emailing them, they responded with an overwhelming, "YES!"

Not only was our livestream a wonderful success, but women asked for more. They wanted to hear from more women about their YouTube journeys. They longed to learn what women in different niches, and from diverse races, were doing to find success. These women wanted help in handling the struggles, and advice on how female entrepreneurs dealt with confidence, trolls, and self-doubt from a female perspective.

I knew I didn't have the bandwidth to make this into another YouTube channel, but I did think these stories needed telling. Primarily because these were stories I (and other women) wanted to hear. So, I went back to Tubebuddy and proposed partnering to make Women of YouTube into a podcast.

The Women of YouTube podcast launched on October 15th, 2019, at Vidsummit. From day one, the response was amazing. Women flocked to their podcast players every week to hear the latest from women of all backgrounds and channels, answering the question, "Why YouTube?"

This brand partnership became one of my all-time favorites. And that is because I not only have the love and support of the Tubebuddy team to create this podcast. It is also because I am getting paid to do something I absolutely adore, that is, to tell stories. I can't get enough of these women, their knowledge, experiences, and unfiltered kindness. To me, this defines the perfect partnership. I would make this podcast even if I weren't getting paid, because I adore the product. I was a user before becoming a partner, and that, in my opinion, is what makes for the best relationship.

Sendible

Back in 2010, I asked my dad if he could program something for me. I needed a way to auto-post content onto Facebook and Twitter, so I wouldn't have to do it manually every day for my growing customer list. My dad was a computer programmer, so I didn't think it would be a big thing for him to do. He emailed me back a couple of days later with a link and a message saying, "just use this." The link was to Sendible.com, and on July 19, 2010 I quickly became a customer. It cost $12 a month to use, which was a big commitment for my bootstrapping startup!

To this day, it is the ONLY social media software I will use. I spent my time in the trenches experimenting and playing with other tools. But no matter how fancy, promising, or easy they all claimed to be, Sendible has always stood true as the best tool for the job.

In August of 2018, I put together a fancy new set (we are talking Canon m50 camera, Rode mic, three-point lighting, and a background that I spent months cultivating in my head. I wanted to start showing off the tools I loved and used for planning social media content. These tools would help me to continue helping my audience. I recorded a video titled "How to

Use Sendible - The Best Social Media Management Tool," and I officially showed up on Sendible's radar.

That December, I reached out to Martine, the Brand Advocacy Coordinator at Sendible, to see if they would be interested in sponsoring my new Live Streaming Podcast. I was still going strong with the Marketing for Your Boring Business, but in October, pivoted to recording the podcast as a Live Stream. My goal was for Sendible to sponsor my show, launching our partnership.

My email led to a Zoom meeting with Gavin, the CEO of the company, and Nico, the head of marketing. After discussing the show and its goals, we agreed that Sendible would give me a free account, and I would use an affiliate link to promote the company during the show. It was my first sponsorship, so I was super excited to save money on something I was already paying for but making money from the affiliate program.

As our relationship continues growing, Sendible and I have worked together on different projects. We've consulted on doing a brand party during Social Media Marketing World. We started a Facebook Group for Sendible customers. I've been a guest on their podcast, and they on mine, and in general, we've become friends. I am continuing to find ways to work more and more with Sendible. I truly love their product, their dedication to their mission to help people tell their stories, and giving world-class customer service.

Now my next goal is to (wo)man their YouTube channel. (Seriously, Gavin, what's taking so long on this? *wink*)

When you bring together a fan and a product they love, the success that comes from that is truly amazing.

Crystal Hammond
Live Streaming Local Celebrity

Crystal Hammond is the owner of Sitter for your Critter and has been a pet professional since 2008, working with thousands of pet owners, and has grown her pet-sitting business to an evaluation of over $500,000 by buying her competitors, cultivating an amazing team, and innovative marketing tactics.

I've had Sitter for your Critter since 2008. I started with probably maybe five clients. I was working the front desk at a gym while growing my client list to what is now almost 6,000 clients. Sitter for your Critter is a dog walking, pet sitting, pet taxi, overnight care pet care company that loves on your pets when you are working or on vacation.

So, leading into 2018, I had done all of your typical marketing stuff, like your email campaigns. I did a lot of old school marketing where I would do doorknob hangers and stuff like that. And so, I wanted to try something new and had a 10-year anniversary coming up. So, I had the idea to do a contest around our 10-year anniversary. And I wasn't really sure how I was going to run this contest, but I decided that one big component of running this contest was going to center around live streaming. I wanted to do something that would allow for my clients, and prospects, to see me to build trust and also get more interactive engagement. I was going to be able to do so many more things and different types of things throughout the year if we were live streaming.

I liked for the clients to be able to see me, because our business is basically based on trust. You have to know that the person is not a crazy person, because we're in your home. Not only is it super personal and intimate, we're in your bedrooms, in your living rooms, in your kitchens, but we're also taking care of your family members. So, people really, really need to know that we're not crazy and that we are who we say we are.

So, with live streaming, it gives you a chance to actually look at the person, actually hear them speak, and you can kind of get to know who they are. So, in my industry, when you are trying to build that trust factor, live streaming is kind of a no brainer.

My Live streams were wildly successful. I was able to grow my business and get new leads in a time when my industry never has growth. And it made me a local celebrity in my town. I remember getting recognized in the drive-through of Dunks (Dunkin Donuts for your non-New Englanders) by the woman who gave me my drink and being approached in the grocery store to chat. It was amazing and the exact results I wanted.

What really made my Live streams next level successful was by partnering with local businesses to not only give additional value to my audience but also to give attention to theirs. When I did a live stream with a local house-sitting company about different ways my audience could clean their house from fur, smells, and other not-so-obvious pet related problems she was so excited to share with HER audience. This resulted in more business for both of us because we showed up and gave value.

By the end of my contest, I was able to close business with over 500 new customers to do dog walks, over-nights, and pet visits by the end of 2019. I got to the point where I knew every time I went Live, I would make sales.

MY MOMENT OF INNOVATION

Just press record. Just do it! It's not going to be perfect and it shouldn't be perfect. My first live was a hot mess, but I showed up and connected. It should not be perfect. Just press record. And you know what, maybe nobody will watch you. Who cares, but just do it. Keep practicing, keep getting better and the business will come. That is hands down my best piece of advice to anyone. Just go press record!

Streamyard

When I switched the Marketing for Your Boring Business podcast to a live show, I was ready to level this podcast up. My YouTube channel was really taking off at this point (thanks to that clear vision and purpose), but my podcast was getting very few downloads. My thought process was, if I could make it into a killer live show, that would help amp it up.

But if there is one detail I care most about, it's how something looks. I want a nice-looking live stream. The problem was that some of the budding new tools out there were just too complicated to use. Don't get me wrong, I am not afraid of tech and I can hold my own when it comes to computer stuff. These tools were too "extra" for my needs. The only extra I could handle in my life at this time was guacamole!

I recently started a hand-on course on how to make a killer live streaming show. I designed it to help me grow my business. While I was working diligently on the course, I met a bloke from the UK named Graham. Graham became my live streaming friend, and he suggested I check out Streamyard.

Once I finally got into the tool, I realized Streamyard was exactly what I needed! They had the one, easy-to-use solution I needed to turn my live streams from a girl in her bedroom into a real show, with overlays. I could make beautiful, television show quality graphics and overlay them onto the live stream. The graphics would show my name, my guest's name, websites, images, and more.

I quickly became obsessed with this tool and told EVERYONE about it. At the time of this writing, my YouTube video about how to use Streamyard is my #1 most popular video, with more than 70,000 views.

Streamyard was a lot harder to crack. I spent months and months trying to connect with the company's founders, about how we might work together. But when you are a startup and a developer, it is easy to get lost in the day-to-day work and postpone brand partnerships and marketing opportunities.

I finally got the privilege of meeting Geige, one of the Streamyard founders, at Social Media Marketing World 2020. I know so many of my stories include SMMW, but this event is a big part of my story. We did a wonderful interview together for my YouTube channel. Better yet, I finally got to plant the seed with him that I wanted to work together somehow. Shortly after our encounter, he reached out to me about their new affiliate program, which of course, I signed up for immediately. I also used the opportunity to connect with him directly. I was able to schedule a call with him and show him some love in my forward, no-BS Desiree kind of way.

I laid it out for him. I told him that even though Streamyard is experiencing an amazing surge in business, he needs to keep (or start) marketing. He can't just ignore PR requests, potential sponsorships, or managing the new affiliate program. I should add that this conversation happened during the first few weeks of the Covid-19 pandemic when everyone was livestreaming everything.

And I told him that he shouldn't be doing the marketing, but that I should be.

On a side note, I was insanely inspired by my encounter with a Streamyard competitor at SMMW2020 (yes, them again). I met their new marketing person and talked with one of their founders about bringing her onboard. I told Geige how instrumental she had been in managing all the little marketing things, so they could focus on what they do best, which was developing their tool.

Geige was sold. I got an email a couple of days later, laying out the scope of the work he would like me to help them with, and a proposed dollar amount.

Brand partnerships take time to develop and should start with brands you truly love. It also doesn't matter what kind of business you have. If you can give value to someone and they are willing to kick back to you, do it! What matters is that you are helping others by providing a voice to a service that they don't have.

That is because no one has your voice, or uses the product as you do, or cares in the way that you do.

MOMENT OF INNOVATION

I am now the breadwinner for my family. It isn't easy, but I am happy to know my family's financial success starts and stops with me. My husband has been able to take the steps towards healing his mind and soul without the looming fear of being taken from his family or worrying that he has to do something because the family needs it. All we need is for him to be better and that will happen one day at a time.

It is so interesting to me how often desperation can dictate our decisions. My moments of desperation came from my life choices not going the way I had planned, yet they brought out my most inspiring and innovative solutions. Desperation gets such a bad rap as a bad thing, when really it is just another way to learn and grow, just like failure.

Personal and professional growth requires constantly reaching beyond your capabilities. It requires being pushed into situations where you choose whether to adapt, overcome, and innovate or accept your fate of dying a slow terrible death. (For some really dramatic cases of not being innovative and stubborn see Blockbuster and JC Penny.)

Innovation from Desperation

When my husband came to me in his moment of pure desperation, I chose to be innovative and problem solve, put together a plan, and make it happen. Innovation is useless without the "making it happen" part.

This lesson can really be applied to anything. If something isn't working, make a plan to fix it.

If your Facebook reach is tanking, problem-solve through it, put together a plan, and make it happen.

If your YouTube videos aren't performing the way you want them to, problem-solve through it, put together a plan, and make it happen.

If you are losing clients, problem-solve through it, put together a plan, and make it happen.

If you are struggling with accomplishing your goals, problem-solve through it, put together a plan, and make it happen.

If you can't seem to master that perfect face contouring, well, just watch YouTube videos until you figure it out.

You can see where I am going with this.

But know this, an idea and a plan are completely useless if you are not willing to make it happen. Ideas and planning are the easy part; it is the doing that is the real test of your desire to be innovative.

Desiree Martinez

What was a moment where you were making it happen for your business? Tag me in this story with @mrsdesireerose with #shareyourinnovation on social media.

CHAPTER 14
THEN, PANDEMIC

We moved to Phoenix in July 2019, and I had a couple more months until the full financial burden of our family was going to be on my shoulders. It felt so big to me, which is crazy, because I was the breadwinner before we went into the Air Force. However, I think the fact that we had kids now made it seem a million times more stressful.

While getting settled into our rental home, I was starting to dig into my three-part strategy. Then, the worst thing that could have happened at that time occurred. I lost about half of my clients.

More and more clients began dropping off, suddenly deciding to move their marketing in-house. There were no outside factors, such as a weak economy; clients were not finding value in my services anymore. I was pulling my hair out because this couldn't have happened at a worse time. I was less than 90 days away from being financially responsible for FOUR people (and two dogs.).

I felt like such a loser. I started asking myself "Why couldn't I make entrepreneurship work for me?" I had received countless glowing accolades and had case studies that showed how my social media marketing services helped clients' businesses. I was involved in a mission that was assisting military spouses around the world. So, why were people leaving?

I dove into the analytics for every client. I researched what was happening in the industry, and I asked customers why they were choosing to leave. They all pointed to one answer: our service wasn't working anymore.

Posting every day on Facebook and Twitter was like dumping buckets of water into the ocean. It wasn't doing anything to get our customers noticed. The custom graphics were pretty, but the industry was leaning away from branded content and turning more toward lifestyle photography and video. As for that $25 ad budget, I might as well have been flushing the money down the toilet. The $25 wasn't converting anything for pages anymore. The way effective ads were being done had changed. The entire process required more time and attention than merely hitting Boost.

It was all my fault. The complications of my life, the stress, the mental health struggle, all the life finally caught up to my business and it wasn't pretty.

I had to pivot and FAST! I had started offering YouTube management at the beginning of 2019. That service for clients involved editing videos, optimizing them for YouTube, and even including a blog for each video. I wanted to help clients get found by Google and YouTube search engines. I knew the power of video from my own experience, and I wanted to offer something better to a few customers.

But, I wondered, what if we included it as a part of our social media services?

After much research, finding the right tools, and training the team, we rolled out a new social media package and pricing structure in September of 2019. It was four years after I started All-In-One. Stephen had been asking and asking me repeatedly to raise my prices, but I couldn't seem to get myself there. I had raised our pricing from $125 to $149 about a year into the business, but I was too mentally blocked to do more. But, after looking at the marketing and the quality of the new service we were going to be offering in our new packages, I knew I needed to raise our prices.

The new service included three posts per week to Facebook and Instagram, along with two text-animated (or social videos) per month. Our price for the package was $299. We would no longer offer Facebook ads, and we would now charge an upsell fee for posting on other platforms like Twitter and LinkedIn.

Raising my rates was SO hard for me to do, but I knew it was going to serve my clients better than what we were currently offering. It would also help me with the increased cost of running a business. After all, in the four years since launching, the world had gotten more expensive. Tools began costing more, and it was unrealistic to expect our services to stay so inexpensive when we were offering so much more value.

In the coming months, we signed up clients who didn't bat an eye at the new pricing. I was so relieved that we were going to bring in more revenue for the company. We would be able to meet the goal of replacing my husband's income, so he could focus on the healing he needed and become the person he wanted to be.

Heading into 2020, I was on fire, working hard core on my three big goals. I had more than 12 speaking gigs planned between January and May and was getting more opportunities presented to me weekly.

I was working with one of the biggest skateboarding brands in the world on their content strategy. That effort was converting a crazy amount of views and revenue to them, while also getting more clients for All-In-One. I decided to invest in myself by bringing a virtual assistant on board. The VA would help with the distribution system I had begun developing at the end of 2019 for customers and my brand. That distribution system was also one of the topics I was going to be speaking on that year. So, I had to implement it myself because if I won't drink my own Kool-Aid, how could I expect anyone else to?

The Women of YouTube podcast hit 5,000 downloads by its tenth episode. My YouTube channel was snowballing after leveling up again. I had added closed captions, improved thumbnails, and utilized Tubebuddy's new SEO optimization tool. AND, I had started writing this book that is in your hands right now!

I was heading into Q2 of 2020, ready to blow up my personal brand. I intended to expand my offerings into a do-it-together social media service, centered around video marketing, and begin maximizing affiliate marketing opportunities.

Desiree Martinez

COVID-19

On March 6th, I got a text message from my very best friend saying that she has lost more than $14,000 over the past three weeks due to the Coronavirus. Since the end of January, my husband had been watching what was happening with the Coronavirus. He kept talking about how worried he was about it. To ease his mind, we did some things to prepare. We bought a deep freezer, which was something we wanted, and made multiple trips to Costco to build out a dry good pantry. We bought extra meat, flour, sugar, and Clorox wipes. It was stuff we usually got, but we bought a little extra. Stephen even asked me to wear a mask on my upcoming flight and to take Clorox wipes and hand sanitizer with me. So, I did.

But on March 9, it was as if a switch flipped in the United States, and suddenly all things Coronavirus were everywhere. There was a run on toilet paper, hand sanitizer, face masks, and cleaners. There were shortages everywhere. There was much debate about whether this virus was similar to the flu or a more deadly pandemic. Scientists were fighting to be heard through the political conversations. Governors in each state began closing down facilities and canceling events with each day. Schools moved online. Life was getting really scary.

The entire country went into lockdown and then

panic over getting the disease morphed into an economic conversation as the economy began collapsing. Restaurants and retail stores were forced to close, and companies that could keep going were having their employees work from home. Millions of people started filing for unemployment, and the jobless rate soared to levels not seen since the Great Depression of the 1920s.

The Federal Government tried to do what they could by offering Paycheck Protection initiatives, an economic stimulus check to every American, and more. Companies offered discounts, while more businesses began using delivery services and offering only online purchases. In a very short time frame, a global pandemic was changing the world.

My best friend ended up closing the doors of her pet sitting business two weeks after she sent me that text message. She went from managing the pets of more than 6,000 families to only six. SIX! And, those six were the pets of medical professionals.

My business took a hit. I lost about half my work or saw it reduced because some people had no way of making money. My big plans for travel and growth were flushed down the toilet. We moved my in-laws in with us because they were dealing with health complications and didn't have the physical ability to isolate. Stephen and I were sleeping on a guest bed in our living room. Our two small kids were home all day, along with two elderly adults, and three dogs. Six of us (plus the dogs) were all crammed together in a small 1,200 square foot house. The house had already become too small, even before the added chaos.

As was the case with many families, emotions were high, and stress was off the charts. What made me the craziest was that I felt like I had already lived through an economic trauma and did NOT want to do it again. Twelve years ago, the Great Recession of 2008 put me on the path I was currently on, and I had determined then that I did not want to struggle like that ever again.

And, I didn't want others to either.

I had to do something to help businesses like that of my best friend, and so many others. Many of them were facing bankruptcy, furloughs, debt, and so much more. But what could I do?

Digital Inspiration Summit

Many of the affected businesses were small business owners. These are the same businesses that All-In-One is here to help! They are the restaurant owners making food and tending to guests, pet sitters watching those fur babies while mom and dad are away on a trip, and the retail owners. The latter are busy ordering inventory and trying to stay up with trends in their industries.

These business owners know how to do their jobs, but now what are they supposed to do when they are shut down? Go to the internet and magically make money? NO! They needed help. That's when the idea came to me. I would put on an online summit to show these struggling business owners how they can make money. I would help them generate income so their business could survive this pandemic, and maybe even come out on top.

I tapped into my network hardcore and asked all the right people to do a pre-recorded session about their area of expertise. I wanted them to show a business owner how he or she could utilize that knowledge in their business. I was able to bring 30 speakers together to talk about every marketing area I could imagine. I had podcasting, live streaming, YouTube, video marketing, membership, email, referral marketing, and more. I even included bonus topics like financial analysis, digital and legal, writing a book, things that people don't think they need to know, but actually need help implementing.

I put this together in a month and offered it for free.

Yep, FREE! Why? Because people needed help trying to make money, and this wasn't the time to sell to them. To help make this even more successful, I was able to get some sponsors on board. They helped ensure that these business owners had the right tools to move forward. Because of the sponsors' generosity, businesses received the help they needed to add revenue to their struggling companies.

We had hundreds of people sign up. Those people needed that help and got it!

Ecamm: Leap Into Live Streaming Bootcamp

Katie Fawkes is a dynamic marketing leader and strategist of over 15 years with a proven record of building and growing brand awareness, driving traffic, and growing customer recognition. She heads up Marketing at Ecamm Network, a leader in Mac software.

Ecamm Live is an all-in-one live streaming production platform for Mac. It allows anyone to create professional-quality, live stream broadcasts or pre-recorded video content, but like any new tool, there is a learning curve. We saw a need to educate people about the service and how to use it, so we decided to put on a free webinar.

With the recent COVID-19 outbreak, we saw an increase in people wanting to learn how to use Ecamm Live, and how to effectively live stream for business. It's one thing to just go live. It's something entirely different to know the strategies behind it all so that you can be successful. We knew that we could offer valuable, helpful content that could make a big difference in people's lives.

Ironically, we had already planned everything out in February before COVID-19 really hit (at least here in the U.S). I will say that COVID-19 definitely helped drive more attendees because (sadly) many businesses needed to quickly move their businesses online and needed to learn new tools and strategies. Thankfully, we were there to help! The response was overwhelming. We had a goal of 1,000 attendees and ended up with over 6,000.

Ecamm ran the Leap into Live Streaming Bootcamp in partnership with Stephanie Liu from Lights, Camera, Live. Together, we had a solid list of experts whom we had worked with in the past or were learning from ourselves. So, it was a matter of creating a good list of the questions that we knew that people were asking. From there, we formed topics around those questions and found the right speaker/session for each.

We also partnered with Annette at Easil to create some beautiful graphics and leveraged our speakers to help us promote. We built out a promotional calendar that we shared with everyone, so we all had the same talking points.

Our sessions were organized from beginning to more advanced topics. So, someone could flow through the three days of content and learn everything they needed to know. Or, they could decide they wanted only to grab the beginner's or expert-level content.

MOMENT OF INNOVATION

Always start with the need and think about how you can help other people. The rest will grow from there. The one other thing I would note is that I've always gotten by "with a little help from my friends."

MOMENT OF INNOVATION

During times of struggle, ask yourself, how can I help?

Throughout the pandemic, there have been so many people trying to sell their services, suggesting that what they have to offer will help people through these hard times. IMHO, this type of marketing is so tacky. Like, slow your roll dude, this is not helping anyone!

Oh, and I swear if I ever hear the words "during these uncertain times" one more time, someone is getting punched in the face.

My husband always says I am a bleeding heart, and that I am not aggressive enough to close sales. But my compassion and desire to help people is what makes me a good person. I guess if I have to choose between being aggressive (but feel slimy about it) versus being a good person (even if it costs me money), I always choose to be a good person. And, it is my sincere hope that you do, too.

I don't know how the pandemic affected you, your business, or your family, but I know how it shook mine to its core. Just when I thought dealing with what we now know to be PTSD was bad, this pandemic definitely is a solid contender fighting in the ring of misery. But even through those incredibly dark times, I focused on the light.

And what's more I didn't keep my struggles to myself. It would have been so easy to hide my pain and frustrations and put on a smile for social media, but I knew that my real experience was going to help more people than being positive. I was incredibly open on social media about how I was feeling and how I was struggling and the love and support I got in return, not only helped me heal, but also proved that people don't want your perfectly filtered, happy-go-lucky crap. They want you real, raw, and imperfect.

How are you being real, raw, and imperfect with your personal brand? (Trust me I know it's hard, but essential!) Tell me about it by tagging me @mrsdesireerose with #shareyourinnovation on social media.

CONCLUSION

Social media has changed the world in ways we could never have imagined. One day, we were all just using payphones, watching commercials, and eating our bagels without taking any pictures of it. We gave no thought that there was a different, faster, or social sharing way of living our lives.

Now we are connected to more information than ever before. We can have relationships with people we have never met in person. We have access to celebrities and brands at the touch of a button. We can become famous by showing up on camera to strangers. We can manipulate algorithms, pay for attention, and create our own empires from our bedrooms.

But while you are busy clicking away and working out those thumb-scrolling muscles, don't forget how much impact you can have on the world. What you say matters. What you post can affect someone. What you share can become someone's new opinion. How you present yourself and your story could change someone's life.

Make sure who you are online is who you are in real life. You aren't helping anyone, including yourself, by just showing your highlight reel.

This is my story that I knew I needed to share, because I truly feel there is a huge gap in the stories marketers and business professionals tell. I want you to know that you are not alone. It is okay that you are struggling or have struggled. I want you to know that it is okay to cry, and to be completely sidelined by life, it is okay if you have or are going through trauma.

It is okay, because I believe you are impossibly amazing.

From your moments of desperation, you will find innovations. You will find the answer and work towards it even if it takes more out of you than you realize you have. I want you to have everything you have ever wanted and then reach for more.

But you need to tell your story in all its messy, relatable glory. That is the secret to social media success.

Since 2010, I have watched algorithms change, platforms start, evolve, and die. I have seen trends and controversy and victories and hardships. I have seen the world come together and tear each other apart one post, one movement, one share at a time.

But the root of everything comes down to stories - your story. Your story is capable of showing someone who is desperately low and struggling how to overcome their struggles and find inspirations in themselves.

Social media is such an amazing and powerful platform for you to inspire the world. Stay true to who you are, don't filter yourself, be honest with yourself and your followers, solve problems, put together a plan, and then make it happen.

Be the inspiration for others' desperation, one post at a time.

ACKNOWLEDGMENTS

Books take a lot of work, but life is filled with amazing people that make your story complete and your life full with joy, happiness and adventures.

To my husband Stephen. The pages of our journey are always turning, bringing us new adventures, challenges, opportunities, and purpose. You motivate and inspire me every day and I am so honored and lucky to have you in my corner through it all.

To my kids, you guys are just so weird and I hope you stay that way forever. Please never stop asking for snuggles, singing loudly in the car, and challenging me to be a better mom.

It should be noted that this book would NOT exist without my mom. She has always, and I mean ALWAYS, been my biggest cheerleader. Every idea, everything I did, every mistake I made, she has been there smiling and cheering me on. I love you Mom, there is nothing else I can say but thank you.

Dad, sorry if this never makes it on to any best-seller list (please readers, don't let this happen! Just leave a review on Amazon, easy!). But know that while you are a total PITA, I wouldn't want you any other way. I am so grateful for the work ethic you instilled in me and teaching me to never accept average. I love you very much.

Dan & Karen, your unwavering friendship, love, prayers, and support all these years has shown me that family isn't just what you are born with, but is also who you chose to spend it with. You are just everything right in this world and I can't wait to watch us all get old and weird(er) together. Zoe and Daniel, thanks for letting me be your Auntie and for being such awesome cousins to my kids.

Crystal, you are my ride-or-die! Thank you for all the pep-talks, encouragement, support, and endless phone calls and texts. Having a business bestie is the greatest thing anyone can do for another lady in business and I am grateful to you every day. I love you and Ty-Ty so very much.

Big ups to everyone who put up with me through this crazy project and deadline. Dave, my editor, Tisha, who did my forward, all my friends who wrote me letters of encouragement, and everyone who was kind enough to give me praise to help make this book a success.

And to everyone who has been on this social media journey with me, thank you for every click, view, comment, share, and like. You not only have helped give me a life I never thought possible, but driven me to keep creating for you.

You all are IMPOSSIBLY AMAZING!

QUICK FAVOR

So, did you like this book?

I really appreciate your reading my book. It was all the feels getting it done, but I hope that you enjoyed our time together.

May I ask a quick favor?

Would you mind leaving an honest review of this book on Amazon? Reviews are the best way to help others find this book.

You can just do to the link below to share your thoughts.

You are impossibly amazing and I am so grateful to you!

www.MrsDesireeRose.com/LeaveAReview

ABOUT THE AUTHOR

Desiree Martinez is the CEO of All-In-One Social Media, award winning social media marketer, and nationally acclaimed speaker on video and content marketing. Her YouTube channel has surpassed 100s of thousands of views by helping businesses grow with better social media and content marketing. She has built a mission-driven, do-it-for-you social media marketing agency to put military spouses to work anywhere they are stationed around the world that has grown into a six-figure business. Additionally, her podcast and online community, Women of YouTube, brings together female YouTubers to inspire, educate, and support other women to create on YouTube.

She lives in Phoenix with her husband, two kids, and two dogs, Kara and Vinnie.

Connect with her at www.mrsdesireeford.com.

Let's share your story with the world!

With my Do-It-Together Content Marketing membership we will build a content marketing road map that actually works by doing less with more! I want to get you off that spinning wheel of always creating, always posting, and never getting results.

With just one problem solving video per month, you will be able to create a foundation for all your marketing each month, create supporting content, tell your story to share your messaging, all with quality content to connect with your audience, build a community, and accomplish more in less time. And I will be with you every step of the way!

What are you waiting for?!

Stop struggling with your social media and content marketing and start creating content that gives value, gets leads, and builds a community for your brand!

Visit
www.MrsDesireeRose.com/Membership

NOTE FROM THE AUTHOR

The events depicted in this book are related to you as I remember them. Other people in my life may have a different recollection. I did my best not to misrepresent any person, event, or organization in any way. In some cases, I chose not to use an individual's full name or real name so as to not put them in jeopardy or harm's way.

Made in the USA
Columbia, SC
30 August 2020

17983571R00128